Perfectly Still

A Journey Through the Heart of Loss to Love

PATRICIA B. MORAN

STATION HILL

BARRYTOWN, LTD.

Published by Station Hill / Barrytown, Ltd.
in Barrytown, New York 12507.

E-mail: publishers@stationhill.org
Online catalogue: http://www.stationhill.org

Station Hill Arts is a project of The Institute for Publishing Arts, Inc., a not-for-profit, federally tax exempt organization in Barrytown, New York, which gratefully acknowledges ongoing support for its publishing program from the New York State Council on the Arts.

Cover photo and design by Susan Quasha.

Library of Congress Cataloging-in-Publication Data

Moran, Patricia B.
Perfectly still : a journey through the heart of loss to love / Patricia B. Moran
p. cm.
ISBN 1-58177-063-4 (alk. Paper)
1. Moran, Patricia B. 2. Spiritual biography—United States. 3. Bereavement—Religious aspects. I. Title.

BL73.M66 A3 2000
248.8'66—dc21

00-042909

Manufactured in the United States of America

Acknowledgments

Many lives were impacted by the experiences described in this book. I am honored by the opportunity to tell this story, and I hope I have captured something in the telling that will seem true to everyone who was directly involved.

The persons with whom I shared these experiences seem naturally to fall into categories based on their generation. Perhaps this is fitting for a book about deaths that occurred in the embrace of family. Sarah's parents, Jane and Bud Mechling, my mother's siblings, Jack, Dick and Ted Anderson and Dottie Antman, and my mother's friends fall into the first generation. To all of you: thank you for your warmth and guidance. My siblings, Mary Moran, Jon Moran, Peggy McGinn, Peggy's husband Brian McGinn, Sarah's sisters Julie and Nancy Reynolds, Sarah's husband Patton Boyle, and my friend Linda Eddy are in my generation. It is impossible for me to separate this time from my relating to each of you, and for that I am forever grateful. Finally, to the youngest generation, Lynde and Margie Nanson, Zach and Corey Moran, Katelyn McGinn, and Hillary and Ivana Reynolds-Boyle: you were, and continue to be, the best teachers of all about the true nature of love.

There are also persons whose presence and support are inextricably woven into the writing of this book. Patton, from beginning to end, was an inexhaustible source of encouragement, insight, and editing! All three of my siblings contributed in valuable ways. Mary was the first person I called when I was stuck, and she gave her very capable assistance with great generosity. Jon was a non-stop source of enthusiasm and creative energy. Peggy was the most supportive and loving friend a person could ever have. Julie has become a dear friend. Marcella Brady shared her love and her deep insights about dying gleaned from years as a hospice nurse. My children, Zach and Corey, have lived with me writing this book for so long, it has become a part of our family. You both truly are my pride and my joy. It does not matter how long it is between phone calls and e-mails to Hillary and Ivana, we always pick up where we ended the time before, with the most precious and open love. I hope some day this book helps you know something more about your mom.

In addition, many persons (so many I have lost track) read drafts of this book and provided insights and encouragement that truly nourished me. I thank you all.

Finally, my heartfelt thanks to George and Susan Quasha and Chuck Stein of Station Hill / Barrytown, Ltd. The book couldn't have found a better home.

For everyone whose love assists the dying in passing from this life

Introduction

In the summer of 1995 both a student of mine, Sarah, and my mother died. Sarah died of leukemia and my mother died of a brain tumor. Despite the deep loss I experienced with these deaths, they brought me to a profoundly different understanding of living. This book tells the story of what I learned.

—1—

"Have you heard about Sarah Reynolds?" Mary asked as she stepped into my office.

I could tell from the tone of her voice that the news was bad. I put my pen down and turned my swivel chair a quarter turn to face her. "No, I haven't heard anything. What is it?" I replied anxiously, looking up to meet her eyes.

"She has acute leukemia."

"Oh my God," I said as my shoulders slumped and I stared at Mary in disbelief.

I flashed to the day, the previous year, when Sarah had visited the department at Oregon State University where I was a professor. She wanted to see if the department would meet her needs for a graduate program in human development. We sat in the department lounge on a couch by a window. I liked her immediately. She was serious and intense but genuinely open. I imagined she had led a life full of diverse experiences and had challenged and rejected the parts of mainstream life that didn't suit her. I liked that about her and thought I would enjoy having her as a student. She told me she had two young children and a husband and was worried about finding a balance between school and family. I told her I could certainly relate, having gone through graduate school myself with two infants, only a few years before.

I asked about her husband's work, wondering what a move from Maine, where they were currently living, to Oregon would mean for him. I was totally taken aback when she told me he was an Episcopal priest.

You are married to a priest? I had said to myself as my mind did a quick rewind to the priests that had been part of my childhood. It seemed enticingly incongruent that Sarah was married to a man of the cloth.

Either Sarah's different than she seems, I had thought, *or her husband is a different kind of priest than I've had contact with, or maybe my associations with organized religion are so old that I am out of touch with what religion can be.*

I had felt an odd kind of energy, wanting to know more and wanting to meet her husband. When our conversation ended, we shook hands and I told her I hoped to see her in the fall.

"She found out about it in a horrible way," Mary continued. "She went to the student health service because she was feeling tired. They did a blood test and she waited for the results. Sarah heard the nurse say something like, 'Oh no!' Sarah called Joanne to tell her she would be late to work. When Joanne answered, Sarah couldn't speak so she handed the phone to the nurse and the nurse told Joanne what was happening. Joanne went over to the Health Services until Sarah's husband could get there."

I could feel myself beginning to go numb. It was all too much to feel and to comprehend. Two young children, about the same ages as my children. How will she talk to her children? What would I do? How can life change so suddenly? My eyes filled with tears.

Mary said, "I know," as she shook her head and looked to the floor.

When Mary left, I turned back to my work. Holding pen above paper, I stared at the white wall in front of me. At that precise moment, I felt an internal sensation like a sliding door being shut. After the door slid to the end of its track, I felt comfortably distant from feelings about Sarah's condition and returned to recording grades, oddly happy to be doing this redundant task I usually dreaded.

The next few days strong emotion stirred behind the door. Then it began to knock, at first politely then, ignored, more insistently. Its message became clear: call Sarah. Unable to disregard the persistent emotion, I began to hold debates in my head about calling Sarah. I wanted to call and offer support. But I would counter these feelings by telling myself that I did not know Sarah very well or that Sarah would want privacy at a time like this. I could have a conversation with myself about all that I wanted to say to Sarah, but when I put my hand on the phone, my stomach would tense and I would pull my hand back as if the phone was something to fear.

As weeks passed, the pull toward Sarah and the equally strong fear of having contact began to collide and spin wildly out of control like the crash of hot and cold weather masses preceding a tornado. My internal protective door was shattered by the force of emotion behind it, and I became increasingly wary of these feelings that were out of my control and understanding.

I searched for a way to explain the compelling energy that had entered my life so suddenly. I didn't even know Sarah very well. She had taken one class from me in the fall and our relationship was clearly one of teacher-student. I had known other people who had faced life threatening illnesses. My response to them had been concern, but I had been able to keep the boundaries between my life and their lives separate and clear. Why did this feel so different? Why, as an outsider, did I feel completely invested, as if Sarah were a sister or a life-long friend? Why did my mind wander incessantly to Sarah and her husband and two children whom I had never even met? Whatever the source of this energy, its power, I discovered, was much stronger than any weapon of logic or reason I had at my disposal.

2

May arrived, school was about to end and, despite the hours of conversations with Sarah that had accumulated in my head, I had not contacted her. By then it seemed the months of inaction on my part were a chasm to Sarah too wide to cross. Surely I couldn't call now and wish her well nearly three months after everyone had learned of her illness. What would I say? "Sorry it's taken me three months to call you." Yet the energy I felt concerning Sarah's illness had continued to swell. I wanted just to shake it away and resolve that the next time someone I knew was in serious trouble, I would be brave enough to call immediately. My efforts to rid myself of preoccupation with Sarah, however, failed completely; it was as futile as deciding not to be in love.

It was during this time, a few days after summer vacation had begun, that my father visited me in a dream.

"Dad," I had said under my breath as I woke up and opened my eyes. "Dad?" I had repeated a little louder, wanting him back.

It had been him, his essence, his humor, his wisdom, and mostly his love that I had experienced. Being with him had felt as comfortable and familiar as always except for an eerie lingering knowing that he had been dead for twelve years.

He had started with a kind, warm ribbing of the ways humans distort what is real. He had chuckled in a grandfatherly sort of way about how serious we humans are about things that are not only unimportant, but are, in fact, illusions. He had been gentle and forgiving about my inability to completely comprehend what he was saying, but he also thought it was important that I try to understand that human lives are unnecessarily bound by untruths of our own making.

I had the strong sense as he spoke that, in dying, he had broken through human boundaries and was now somehow a part of everything. Even though I communicated personally with him, I sensed him everywhere. The love I felt from him was complete and all-encompassing. I wanted to dissolve into this love, but I kept coming up against my own barriers of fear and inhibition and wonder. My inability to reciprocate had nothing at all to do with his love, however. His love just was.

Smiling and shaking his head, he told me that humans are often very confused about love. Love is only one thing, not all the different things we try to make it. There are different ways to love but, if love is real, then all the different ways are the same. Love for animals, or places, or lovers, or children, or friends, or family is all the same. All that matters is to experience and to appreciate love. He admonished me to find love everywhere I could and not to worry a whit about who or what it was that I loved. He said love is all there really is.

Then, focusing on me with boundless humor in his sparkling eyes, he said he had found it very funny to discover that the earth from the heavens looks just like the heavens from the earth on a clear night with millions of stars radiating light. The lights on earth visible from the heavens are the love that humans are genuinely experiencing in their lives. At that point, I awoke. I couldn't remember closure, a goodbye.

I lay in bed, curled up under the covers staring ahead. I sensed something important had happened but I could barely touch the experience. A muted, subtle version of the loss ache that had been so familiar after my father's death arose in my gut only to recede and disappear. A sense of joy in my father's message of love flickered momentarily and then died as if extinguished by a breeze. By the time I got out of bed, showered and made breakfast for myself and my children, I had created such an internal distance from the experience that if someone had asked if I could remember my dreams from the night before, I would have replied no.

3

About a week after the dream with my father, I went to a video store in Corvallis, the small college town where I worked. As I was leaving, Sarah entered the store, only a few feet from me. Her head was wrapped in a scarf but otherwise she looked like she always had. My heart pounded and I was filled with the anxiety of being in a situation I wanted frantically to avoid but could not escape.

We looked at each other, my eyebrows raised in surprise, then she smiled warmly and opened her arms to me. I took two steps to her and we embraced. I glimpsed briefly the perspective of two relative strangers meeting by accident but lost this objective truth in a single pull of undercurrent from the ocean of feelings Sarah's illness had given rise to in me. I stumbled stupidly for words; there were too many, but I did manage to ask a couple of simple questions. She told me she was doing well and was hopeful. I said an awkward goodbye and walked to my car light and joyful and tremendously relieved.

We called each other a few times over the next couple of weeks. I found myself asking Sarah questions that seemed to come directly from my heart. I was unaware of processing and selecting the words from my head. How was she feeling? What was hard? What were her fears? I felt a stillness within me when we talked that I had never experienced. It was as if, for the period of time we talked, I was insulated from all other thoughts; we just were. Every time I hung up the phone after our conversations, I would want to remain still, but instead emotion would begin to fill the stillness slowly, rhythmically like a drum beat: something is happening, something big and important, pay attention.

As I began to relate to Sarah, the dream experience with my father seeped into my conscious awareness. At first, I was aware only of the dream's presence, not its content. It was like knowing someone is watching you. Then I began to remember its content. Once I began to remember, the dream returned with great clarity. As if looking at a perfectly focused photograph, I recalled every detail.

Growing up, my father had always been there for me when I really needed him. I wouldn't ask, he would just know. That's how I began to understand why he had visited me. My life was opening to something new. He had come to offer guidance.

4

My first memory of someone dying was when JFK was killed. I was a six year old first grader living in Austin, Texas. We were let out of school early that day to go to a parade to see the president. First he was doing something in Dallas, my mother explained to my twin sister and me on the way to school, then he would come to Austin for the parade.

When we were dismissed from school, I could see our family car in the parking lot at the bottom of the long hill at the back of the school. There were three people inside, my mother, my older sister and somebody else, probably one of my sister's friends. Panting and laughing, I raced down the hill to the car with my twin. When we reached the car, I looked up and saw my big sister's face buried in her hands. Her friend was crying too. My mother's face looked sad and worried. What is wrong? My heart sank as I wondered whether we would be going to the parade. But did my sister and mother want to go to the parade this much? I could be braver than they were being about not going to a parade!

Our mother got out of the car and brought us to her, one arm around each child. "You don't know yet? They didn't tell you?" she asked.

I pulled my face from my mother's skirt and looked up at her face.

"President Kennedy has been shot, honey."

"Will we go to the parade?" I replied.

"No, it has been canceled."

I wanted to ask if that was why everyone was so upset, but some part of me knew better than to ask.

We got into the car and I began to cry, drawn into the sadness that my sister and her friend were expressing. I quickly was trying to learn the rules of what you were supposed to do when someone dies. When you leave a friend's home, you thank the mother for having you over. When someone dies, everyone cries. And yet, despite how far away this death seemed from my life, there was a glimmer of knowing in my child heart that death was about everyone and that it was something I feared.

5

I first met Sarah's husband Patton and daughters Hillary, seven, and Ivana, four, at an end-of-the-school-year party a friend and colleague, Leslie, was having. The girls were active and demonstrative and immediately joined the other children in play. Sarah introduced me to Patton and he sat down in a lawn chair next to me. Between excursions to take care of child needs, we talked for most of the remainder of the party. The energy I had experienced with Sarah also was present in my interaction with Patton, although subdued, a buzzing kind of tension.

Sarah had told me that Patton was a writer and had recently published another book. I asked him about it.

"I took a six month sabbatical a couple of years ago. The whole family traveled around the country in our camper. Each morning I woke up very early and wrote until everyone else was awake. The book just wrote itself, really. Most of the time I wasn't even aware of writing. We spent afternoons seeing the sights. We had a wonderful time."

"That sounds great," I replied, genuinely intrigued.

"Those were some of the best months we ever had as a family," he continued. "Of course Sarah and I had our conflicts. I wanted to wander, she wanted to get some place. But, still, mostly, we all got along well; it was very relaxed. My fantasy is to live that way, with very few possessions, just traveling and writing."

"That would be hard with the kids needing to be in school though, wouldn't it?" I asked.

"Yeah, for now, we'd have to do it just during the summers."

Then he changed the subject and asked me about the town, Eugene, forty-five miles away, where I lived. He and Sarah were thinking of moving there and he wanted to know more about the town. By the end of the party, we had agreed that some time the next week I would show them around Eugene.

Sarah called the day after the party to arrange a date to explore Eugene. The following week Sarah and Patton drove to Eugene and we spent an afternoon driving around town. We had a fun and relaxed time full of the positive energy of blossoming friendship. I made it clear that my sense of direction was suspect at best. Sarah said she thought Patton and I were similar, creative types with our heads in the clouds. She, in contrast, characterized herself as having a lot of common sense.

Sarah and I continued to call each other over the next two weeks. Then she told me she was scheduled to go back to the hospital for another round of chemotherapy. I asked if I could visit her in the hospital and she told me she would like it if I did.

The first time I saw Sarah in the hospital, I went with a mutual friend, Linda. The three of us visited easily. We told Sarah we would stay only a little while because we did not want to wear her out. Three hours later, we were all surprised when we looked at the clock and discovered that I had only a few minutes to get to a meeting.

The next time I visited Sarah in the hospital, a few days later, I went alone. I felt excited but anxious about the visit. It had been a significant relief to make contact with Sarah but I still felt an underlying anxiety I could not explain.

Sarah and I talked about sibling rivalry, the differences between rearing boys and girls, department politics, and Sarah's doctoral program. She asked me if being in the hospital was hard because it reminded me of my father. I told her it had been hard for a few minutes during the first visit but it didn't seem hard now.

Then she asked me why I thought people get cancer. I replied that sometimes cancer is linked to something in the person's environment or in the person's genes but usually no one really knows.

Looking at me seriously, she said she believed that cancer has to do with stress. Beginning graduate school had been extremely stressful with the move across country, a graduate assistantship that was difficult, and she had to take my class in statistics on top of everything else.

I chuckled in response, thinking she was kidding. A quick look at her expression told me she was not. I breathed in sharply and scrambled in my head for a response.

"Gosh Sarah, I guess I don't think the answer is as easy as that," I replied.

She looked at me with a cold, angry expression.

"It's not your fault you know," I blurted, surprising myself with both the forcefulness and the content of my words. "You didn't do anything wrong. It just happened," I continued with a less powerful tone.

As she looked at me, her expression softened; she no longer seemed so far away and angry, but rather absorbed in memory.

"I met Patton in Florida," she said thoughtfully, after a long pause.

She then told me about the beginnings of her relationship with Patton and what had attracted her to Patton.

"I had a different kind of connection with Patton than with other men I've been with. He's a good person, really solid. I wanted a family. It was time for me to be with someone like Patton. I thought I was ready for a family at that point in my life."

"So what about you?" she asked. "What characteristics are you attracted to?"

"Pretty much what you just told me about Patton," I replied smiling.

She described how her relationship with Patton had changed over the years, and how her illness was bringing them closer. Then she wanted to know more about the relationships I had been in. Her questions were uncomfortably insightful and difficult to answer without feeling like I was revealing aspects of myself that were far below the surface.

"You need to show your anger more," she said, looking me straight in the eyes.

"I suppose you're right," I said trying not to squirm under her stare.

"What keeps you from showing your anger?" she continued. "It's not good for you to keep it inside, you know. Say what you think."

"I think this is making me uncomfortable," I said smiling.

"Yeah, but is it making you angry? Probably not. Just my point," she said, breaking into a grin.

By the time I left, our friendship had deepened dramatically. We both knew we could be honest and real with each other. What normally takes much longer to develop in a new friendship was occurring quickly. Neither of us said that if we were to be friends we had better not waste time, but we both knew this to be true.

I visited again two days later.

"It's good to see you," Sarah said smiling when I entered the room.

"Yeah, you too," I replied returning her smile. "So how are you feeling today?"

She caught me up with the latest medical news. Mostly she was tolerating the chemotherapy very well. Some nausea but not too bad.

Then her mood shifted perceptibly to something I did not recognize. She looked intently into my eyes and I wondered what she was about to say.

"You know, if I die I think you and Patton would be good together. I just want to plant that kernel."

I stared back at her with big eyes, locked in her steady gaze. All of a sudden I knew why I had experienced such extraordinary energy concerning Sarah's illness. It was like a story unfolding. Our lives were supposed to cross. I stammered something like, "Oh, Sarah!"

She nodded and said, "Really, I think you would be good together."

I could not find words. I just stared at her.

"Getting close to a dying person could be kind of dangerous," Sarah stated seriously.

My eyes filled with tears and her expression softened.

"Yeah, kind of sets one up for possible loss, doesn't it? Seems worth it, Sarah. I have no doubt it is worth it," I replied, fighting an onslaught of tears.

"I'm glad," Sarah said quietly.

When my visit ended, neither of us knew how to let go. Under normal circumstances we would have embraced, but touching Sarah when her blood counts were very low was not allowed. I stood by the door, left hand on the doorknob ready to leave, and then I turned to Sarah. We looked long at each other. As if having a will of its own, my right hand had moved and now rested over my heart. Still locked in eye contact with me, she did the same. Then I turned and left.

I walked down the hospital hall dazed by the intensity of the connection I had just experienced with Sarah. As I went through the hospital doors and out to the parking lot, I became increasingly aware of a glowing radiant energy that seemed to enter me from a source outside of myself. It carried me lightly to my car.

As I sat in my car, keys in hand, the energy intensified. A feeling of utter euphoria began to seep into and spread through every part of my physical and emotional self. I felt as if I was being absorbed into something enormous, something so grand I was but a microscopic speck in comparison. In being absorbed, I broke through barriers I understood instantly had held me captive all my life but I had never known were there. Suddenly I was free. I was even free of "me." I sat in awe, understanding with complete assurance that the essence of being is loving, peaceful and hopeful.

Then I became aware of an irrefutable, profound sense of knowing that Sarah would die from this disease. The "knowing" was not bad or good, it just was. Somehow, it seemed, the whole universe had shifted slightly so that everything was in perfect alignment. Sarah's death was part of that perfection.

My head voices began to tell me that this was a very strange experience and low level fear began to creep into the expansive joy.

Is something wrong with me? I asked myself. *What is happening?*

I countered these thoughts with evidence that I was normal and sane. Then, suddenly, a thought came to me that collided with the fading euphoria in an internal explosion that left me panicked and frantic to escape what my head had created. Sarah would have to die for the "knowing" to be accurate! What horrible part of me could have allowed myself to feel this tremendous sense of peace and well being if Sarah's dying was linked to these feelings? I leapt to my own defense shouting internally that I had nothing to do with the euphoria. It had come from outside of me and I should not be held responsible. Wanting somehow to get away, I started my car and drove mechanically, so heavy with depression I could barely tell myself to turn my head to merge into the traffic flow.

By the time I arrived at work, the depression had been replaced by mind spinning confusion. How could I make sense of opposites at the same time? How could I want very sincerely for Sarah to live a long life, see her children grow, enjoy life with Patton and yet have experienced utter joy connected to knowing that she would die?

I went to a friend and told her about the conversation I had just had with Sarah at the hospital. Her reaction was that it would be incredible to choose a replacement for yourself in life. I wanted to tell her what had happened in the parking lot, but I felt helpless in finding words to describe the experience or the wreckage of confusion it had left.

I called Sarah at the hospital the next day to check on how she was doing. After greeting me she said, "Hold on for just a minute, I need to tell Patton something."

When she returned she said, "Pat and Patton, sounds pretty good together I'd say."

"Sarah! Jeez, Patton's right there isn't he? Knock it off!" I exclaimed a little amused and mostly horrified at her teasing.

"So how are you doing today?" I asked, wanting to change the topic quickly.

"Pretty well but I'm tired of talking about me. How are you doing?"

I ached to say, "Sarah, something is happening and I don't know what it means. I feel like I am connected to an energy that is different from anything I have ever known and it's exciting and I think I want to know more but I am scared." I was not able, however, to say those words.

6

I was walking my dog back from our neighborhood park not long after the experience in the hospital parking lot when, with a start, I realized that my internal landscape had changed drastically. When I looked inside myself to find guidance and structure, an understanding of the rules by which to live, I found nothing I recognized. Instead, what I saw looked literally like a desert, an endless expanse of motionless sand. Finding myself in this internal desert seemed as real, as lonely, barren and unknown as being transported to an actual desert and left without a compass. I ached with a dull kind of fear; somehow my internal self had changed without my external self even noticing, and now it was too late to do something about it. I wanted to go back to what I knew but I could not find a trace of anything to follow. There was absolutely nothing to do and nowhere to go. I fell to my knees in the middle of my internal desert and stared at where I had, somehow, arrived.

7

My second memory of someone dying occurred a few years after President Kennedy was killed. My twin sister and I were at the University of Texas at Austin taking a swimming lesson. After the lesson we went outside to wait for our mother to pick us up. We heard a "pop pop pop" sound and, laughing, began to run to the sound, thinking there was a fireworks display somewhere near. Then our swimming instructor came running towards us, yelling something we could not understand at first.

"Get back into the building now!"

"But we always wait out here," we protested, feeling that we were being treated unfairly.

"Something's happening and you need to get back inside quickly. Hurry!"

We ran back.

"What's going on?" I asked a friend when we were back inside.

"Somebody's shooting people from the top of the tower."

I felt in that moment like I did when it got very hot in the summer. If you stood still outside in the middle of a sunny summer day, the heat would begin to buzz in your ears. After awhile, if no one disturbed you, the buzz would grow until that's all you could hear and you would feel like you couldn't move. That's how I felt. There was a buzz in my ears, everything inside got quiet, and it seemed I couldn't move.

Our mother called us fifteen or so minutes later. She was calling from one of the buildings the police were shooting from. She said she had to crawl to the phone because everyone had to stay low. She would be there as soon as possible but she had to go because other people needed the phone too. We were to stay right there.

It didn't seem too long before she arrived to pick us up. Lots of hugs and exclamations then in the car with the radio on. I was in the front seat. The radio announcer began to read the names of the people who had been killed.

"Paul Sonatag."

My mother gasped.

"What? No! They didn't say that!" I said angrily to my mother, clinching my teeth, as if she was choosing to hear the unhearable and believe the unbelievable. "They are not right."

"Oh, honey," was all my mother said.

The next time his name was announced, it pierced my wall of denial.

"No!"

By the time we got home, Paul's name had been repeated over and over as had the story of his death. He had run out into the open to help his fiancée who had been shot. He had been killed immediately. One of the announcers said that perhaps it was good he had died because he and his fiancée had been so much in love.

All that summer I watched Paul's brother at the local pool where Paul had coached us in swimming. I wondered and wondered what it would be like to no longer have a brother. Someone you loved could just not be there anymore and there was nothing you could do about it.

8

The day Sarah returned home from the hospital she called wanting to know if I knew where Linda was. Sarah and Linda, a fellow doctoral student and a nurse, had conversed many times about the medical aspects of Sarah's cancer. Sarah had just received news that her leukemia involved a translocation of two chromosomes. She wanted to know if Linda knew anything about translocations and, if not, whether she would go to the medical library and look up information on this type of leukemia.

Linda phoned me a few nights later. Her voice was tense and broken. She had gone to the library and had found a research article on Sarah's particular type of leukemia.

"The news is bad," she said. "The average length of time from diagnosis to death was twenty months. No one in the study survived."

My head filled with a throbbing pulse. The "knowing" was becoming real. I reacted with silence, panicking for a way to refute the results of the study.

"But, these were just people selected for the study, right?" I finally blurted. "There must be a lot more who did survive who weren't in the study."

"The researchers traced down as many medical records of people with this type of leukemia as they could. They weren't selective; everyone they found was included in the study," Linda explained.

"Yeah but the people in the study didn't have bone marrow transplants, right?" I queried anxiously.

"No, some had transplants, others didn't. It didn't matter what their treatment was. If they had this kind of leukemia, they were included in the study," Linda replied patiently.

"Oh God, Linda, what are we going to do?" I asked, my throat constricting with emotion as I lost hope that Sarah somehow was different from those included in the study. "What if Sarah asks what you found?"

"I don't know. I can't lie to her. I hope she doesn't ask. I don't know what to do."

"I don't get it," I said desperately defiant. "How is it that the doctors are telling her she has a chance if there is this information out there saying she doesn't have a chance? Surely they have read the study. They must have some reason to be hopeful."

"I don't know," Linda replied. "But don't make the mistake of thinking doctors know everything."

Then we counted forward from the month of her diagnosis.

"I think she will die in June, middle or late. Don't ask me why, that's just what my gut tells me. It's the part of me that is usually right," Linda stated quietly.

"But that's not even a full year. Linda, that is too soon!"

The Sunday after Linda's phone call, my mother called. Since leaving home for college at age eighteen, I had talked with my mother at least once a week on the phone. She always called Sunday mornings. She insisted on paying for phone calls. Even if I called her, she would tell me to hang up so she could call back.

For years our phone conversations had centered on my career as an academic in the field of human development as well as on the everyday occurrences of both our lives. Her father had been a very well known developmental psychologist and she had grown up surrounded by academics. Then she had married my father who was also a professor of psychology. My mother and father had met when my mother was teaching a correspondence course at the University of Texas that my father was taking. Mom had been so impressed with Dad's answers, she had suggested they meet for coffee. After they married and my mother gave up her career to raise kids, she had become my father's right hand and confidant.

During my childhood, dinner had often been a forum for friendly debate between my parents about some theory in psychology or the meaning of the results of a study recently published. If the discussion was not focused on psychology, it would often be on an interesting fact someone had heard, the definition of an obscure word, or an explanation of some world event. My mother's tireless pursuit of knowledge would often lead to interruptions in dinner as a word was looked up in a dictionary, or a country was located in an atlas.

As I had pursued my career, Mom had been delighted to read my papers, discuss my ideas for research, or talk over department politics. She was the first person I wanted to tell of my successes and my struggles.

I had told Mom about Sarah months earlier in one of our Sunday conversations. Since then, questions from my mother about my career had become secondary to questions about how Sarah was doing. Our mutual concern for Sarah had become a point of deep connection between us. I marveled at my mother's genuine caring for the well-being of people she didn't even know. It seemed she was the one person in the world who knew with absolute certainty how meaningful it was to me to know Sarah and her family. Talking about Sarah had opened up conversations between us about my father's illness and death, aging, and grief, topics that for years had circled our family without landing.

When I told my mother about the study, she was shocked. "Oh Pat! Oh no!" she said breathlessly. "You can't tell her. She needs hope, honey."

My mother's reaction had made my emotional bristles rise. *You're wrong, Mom,* I had thought immediately. *I could tell Sarah. Maybe I should tell her. I certainly would tell her the truth if she asked me. Honesty is good. It is loving to be honest,* I had continued to myself, in touch with some of the issues in my family I had wrestled with as an adult.

But I didn't battle with my mother. The truth was, I wasn't at all sure what was right in this situation.

"I just hope she doesn't ask, Mom," I replied. "She wouldn't ask me anyway. She'd ask Linda. Linda doesn't know what she would do but I have a feeling that Linda would tell her the truth."

My mother was silent and I returned her silence. "Yes," she finally said, "that would be very hard."

—9—

A few days after my conversation with Linda, Sarah called. My gut tensed when I heard her voice, wondering if she had talked with Linda, or whether she would ask me if I had talked with Linda. Instead, she asked if I wanted to be part of a dream group she was starting. The group would consist of four to five members and would meet weekly. Each person would share a dream or an image from a dream and Sarah would lead the group through an interpretation of the dream. Sarah had received extensive training in dream interpretation from some of the best teachers in the world and was experienced in leading groups.

I felt split. I sensed immediately that the group offered an opportunity for personal growth, but I was afraid of putting myself in a situation in which I would be vulnerable in front of strangers. My internal conflict left me responding to Sarah's question with an awkward silence. Before finding a clear response, I began to fumble for words, trying to explain how difficult it was for me to be open in a group setting, especially with strangers, but also how much I would like to participate. As soon as I started speaking, I felt foolish; I was talking to a person fighting to survive a deadly illness about my struggles with being shy. Sarah did not dismiss my obvious conflicting emotions. She said simply that I could, and probably would, feel vulnerable, but the idea of dream interpretation is to honor the dream process itself, not to judge the content of the dream or the dreamer. Dream content, she explained, is about you, but it's also about our connection to a greater whole. I agreed to participate.

I arrived at the first meeting, apprehensive but eager. There were four members plus Sarah. Sarah explained that each person would share a dream or an image from a dream. Sarah would explore the dream with the person, and then she would open the discussion to all members of the group.

As the first group member shared a dream, I found my head racing to analyze its meaning even as the dream was being told. As I listened to responses to Sarah's inquiries about emotions experienced in the dream, colors, persons, objects, however, a meaning unfolded that was entirely different than I had anticipated. My immediate reaction was apprehension mixed with curiosity. The part of my brain that I was used to relying on, the part that worked well logically analyzing information, did not work well doing this. Instead, this process seemed to be about quieting that part of my mind and opening to something else. I felt drawn to the "something else" as my logical mind fought to secure its position of superiority. As the next group member described her dream, I tried to resist interpreting and analyzing, and was immediately rewarded with a calm focus that left me feeling fully present and in tune with the other members.

Each member before me shared a dream she had experienced the previous week. Through the process of interpretation, an issue at the core of each of their lives had been described. I was intrigued by the power of dreams and by Sarah's skills in opening us to their meaning.

In the first dream I shared, I was wandering through a beautiful house that was designed and furnished exactly to my tastes with open spaces and light. It was orderly and serene and I felt wonderfully centered and peaceful. A realtor was in the house with me, showing me around, pointing out special features. I began hesitantly to ask questions about buying the house, not completely believing that I could actually live in such a place.

As the realtor answered my questions, out of the corner of my eye, I noticed a grotesquely deformed ratlike creature. In the dream my heart sank and I felt foolish for allowing myself to believe, even momentarily, that such a peaceful place would really be available to me. I told myself not to look at the creature, but soon other creatures were coming out of the walls and were everywhere. The feeling of the house changed abruptly from serene to horrifying. Then, suddenly, cats appeared and began mauling the creatures in an ugly slaughter. The realtor said the cats would kill all the creatures and then everything would be taken care of. I told myself I could not stand to be a part of the slaughter of these creatures and left immediately with no further interest in the house.

I described the dream with little emotion. Then Sarah began to ask questions about how I felt in the dream, who the other person was, what the creatures were like.

"If this place was so peaceful and good for you, why were you so willing to leave?" she asked.

This question took me by surprise; I hadn't even considered staying. "I just couldn't stand seeing the creatures massacred," I replied.

"What if the cats could kill all the creatures, would you want to live in the house?"

"I don't know. I wasn't at all willing to wait while the creatures were being killed."

"You seem to think it was a bad thing for the cats to kill the creatures."

"Yes. It did seem like something I couldn't stand to witness."

"Do you think it's bad for a cat to kill a mouse?"

"No, but I don't particularly want to watch it get killed."

As I answered her questions, I felt an unnamed, unknown emotion building in my gut. Then, in an explosive burst, I began to cry and then sob. I felt like running from the house but I just sat there, overwhelmed.

"Can you talk about what you are feeling?" Sarah asked when my sobs had quieted.

"It seems so weird, Sarah," I said, inhaling deeply. "It's about your cancer and my father's cancer and how grateful I am that you are dealing with this so openly. He killed himself. The cancer had spread all over his body. My mother came down to the basement where I was sleeping and said she thought Dad was out back. She said she wasn't strong enough to go look. I scrambled out of bed and rushed out the door. He was lying in a pool of blood in the carport. I screamed and ran hysterically into the house. I wasn't screaming because he was dead; I was screaming because I hadn't seen the gun and I thought that he had wandered away from the house, slipped, hit his head, and bled to death. I couldn't stand that," I said crying again.

"I kept repeating to myself like a crazy person that he was supposed to die with us, his family, holding his hand, saying goodbye. After probably less than a minute, I suddenly stopped crying and I went totally numb; I lost all emotion."

My eyes met Sarah's. We just looked at each other.

"I'm really glad I don't feel vulnerable," I said cracking a smile. She and the rest of the group laughed.

"How do you feel?" Sarah asked.

"Exhausted," I replied.

Sarah passed me a box of Kleenex.

"Dreams are powerful," she stated.

—10—

The possibility that Sarah would need a bone marrow transplant had been considered since the diagnosis. The doctors would do everything they could with chemotherapy but a bone marrow transplant had always loomed as a probable necessity

One of the best places in the world to receive a bone marrow transplant was five hours north in Seattle at the Fred Hutchinson Cancer Research Center. Before a transplant could occur, however, a donor had to be located.

Everyone in Sarah's immediate family was tested: her mother, two sisters, two daughters, and Patton. No one was a match. The next step was to use the nationwide computer bank to match characteristics of Sarah's marrow to the marrow of an unrelated person. The process she was told would take a few weeks, if not months. It ended up taking much less time than expected.

At the end of our fourth dream group meeting, in early December, Sarah said there was some business she needed to talk over with the group. A marrow donor had been found, she announced calmly, and she, Patton and the girls were leaving for Seattle at the end of the week. She apologized for needing to stop the group but she hoped we could get back together when she returned.

We were all silent for a moment as this news sunk in. "Sarah!" I exclaimed, breaking the silence and looking at her with an expression that defied her to be so calm. "You are moving to Seattle at the end of *this* week?"

The rest of the group joined in with excited questions. The group's energy was contagious and Sarah became more animated herself. "I know, I can't quite believe it. You know they take you right to the brink of death in the procedure. They try to kill all of the old marrow before you get the new marrow."

"That sounds very scary," I said seriously, meeting Sarah's eyes. Her silence was a reply.

"So they must have found a donor," someone said.

"Actually they found six possible donors. I think they're doing more tests to narrow it down."

"Sarah, this really is great news, isn't it?"

"Yes it is. The odds were in my favor this time."

"I can't believe you are moving to Seattle in a few days. There's a lot to do," I said, understating the enormous task ahead.

"I could talk to my daughter about checking in on your house," one of the group members said. "She's a police officer. I'm sure she'd do it."

"I can come help on Saturday with the packing. I could take the kids somewhere if that would help," I said.

"Yes, that would be good."

"I could keep your cat while you're up there," I continued.

"Oh, I hadn't thought of that. How do you feel about a rat and a gerbil?"

"I could just add them to my farm, no problem. What's another few animals when you already have a dozen?"

Sarah smiled. "Well, maybe you could take them on Saturday. I really appreciate it a lot."

"No problem."

I arrived Saturday morning with Christmas presents for the girls that they opened right away. We spent the day packing and loading the rental truck and cleaning the house. Sarah helped and rested throughout the day.

At one point, Sarah sat down close to where I was working. "I really need to think about what I want to do in the future. It needs to be just mine, not about the kids. It's my defense against the dark side when it comes. During chemo, dark and light can battle and dark sometimes wins. I need to go into this with something to really hang on to so that I can keep in touch with the light."

"That makes a lot of sense to me," I said nodding in agreement.

"What feels right to me is the dream interpretation work. Running groups and attending workshops to learn more. Do you think that's the right direction for me?" she asked.

"Absolutely," I said sincerely. "You have a real talent, Sarah."

Sarah nodded and looked at me intently. "I'm going to go lie down awhile. I'm feeling a bit tired."

"Yes, go lie down. Let Patton and me do the rest."

Towards the end of the day, Sarah left on an errand and Patton and I tackled the task of covering their camper with a tarp. When Sarah returned, we were on the roof of the camper placing firewood in strategic places to keep the tarp in place. She saw us and walked over, smiling broadly.

"I bet it's a lot easier doing this with you than it would be with me.

I'd be arguing with Patton, telling him how to do everything. I bet he likes working with you better!" she said cheerfully.

I shook my head and stuck my jaw out at Sarah. She understood my expression and laughed.

I had to leave around dinner time. After I said goodbye to Patton, Sarah walked me to the door. We embraced and held each other extra long. I heard myself whisper, "I love you, take care," and was immediately embarrassed, feeling like my mouth had betrayed my heart.

"You'll visit us in Seattle, right?" Sarah asked as we let go of each other.

"Absolutely," I said opening the door.

"Bye, thanks for everything."

I just nodded as I turned and walked to the car, unable to speak. Whatever the energy was that was drawing my life to theirs had never felt so powerful.

As I drove away, a thought settled in me that left me so heavy with sadness that I felt unable to move, paralyzed in the depth of the emotion. *Sarah could leave tomorrow and never come back.*

11

My first visit to Seattle was in January, a few weeks after Sarah had made it through the torturous period after intensive chemotherapy and radiation. This treatment was intended to destroy all of her bone marrow and white blood cells in preparation for the donor's marrow. Her throat had been so sore that she barely had been able to swallow or talk. She described the pain of this period as being far worse than childbirth which was the worst pain I could relate to. Despite the physical pain, Sarah made it through the transplant and the period after strong in body and in spirit. All she knew of the donor was that she was a postal worker from the Midwest whose husband was a farmer. Healthy stock we all agreed.

Driving to Seattle felt like going home, like rejoining a part of myself. I wondered at the feeling and then decided just to enjoy it. As had happened many times over the last months, I felt acutely aware of the limitations of the rational, active part of my mind. Until recently, I had believed that part was all of me.

An image flashed into my head. It was in the form of a comic strip. In the first frame I was clinging desperately to a tree, my eyes clinched tightly shut. It was obvious that I was in the middle of some kind of disaster but I couldn't tell what it was. The next frame took a much wider perspective. In that frame I was clinging to a stately tree in the middle of a beautiful park on a clear warm day with birds chirping and deer meandering past. The disaster was all in my head. All I had to do was open my eyes to see the truth.

I burst out laughing and opened the window wide. The wind carried my laughter away.

I arrived late that afternoon at the apartment building where Sarah, Patton and the girls were living. The entire building was for transplant patients and their families. Families from around the world came to Seattle and stayed in this building.

I buzzed the apartment from the security system at the entrance to the building. Patton answered and said he would be right down. He and the girls came off the elevator a few minutes later with a cart to carry my luggage and the boxes of their belongings they had asked me to bring. The girls were excited to see someone from home, and we spent the first half hour opening the small gifts I had brought and catching up on Sarah's condition. She had, just that day, gone back to the hospital because of low blood counts and a low grade fever. Patton said these symptoms probably did not indicate a serious problem and were a part of the process.

I visited Sarah that evening. There was something remarkably comfortable about the hospital floor Sarah was on. It seemed like everything—emotions, physical objects, facial features—was in sharper focus than usual. It was as if there were only room for honesty and clarity in this place where life and death were so closely related. Extraneous details that usually blur our focus did not interfere here. Because it felt so true and real, it also felt safe. I found myself feeling steady and calm and totally in tune with the moment.

Talking with Sarah was wonderful. She made it clear how happy she was to see me, and I felt there was nowhere I would rather be. I caught her up on every interesting detail I could think of from home, and she caught me up on all she had been through. She told me that Patton had performed a communion service with her when the new bone marrow had arrived. The service had been very meaningful to her, not in a way that was connected to religion per se, but rather as a celebration of a new optimism about life. It was a beginning that she wanted to believe in and embrace with all the joy of birth.

"So what do you think about religion?" Sarah asked me with her usual intensity.

After pausing for a moment to gather my thoughts, I replied, "I think I bring so much baggage to it that I can't find the real stuff that's in any religion. There seems to be a part of humans that is drawn to something bigger than us. But when we try to find it in religion, we often feel disappointed because religious doctrine and practices are so polluted with our human limitations. We end up being all wound up in the limitations of our human condition rather than set free to the greater whole that we are a part of."

"Well said," Sarah said, smiling. "I agree. I feel quite certain there is something beyond what we call life. As weird as this sounds, sometimes I'm almost eager to experience what that is," Sarah continued.

"Yeah, it's like maybe you get to know all the answers to these questions," I said, returning her smile.

"Sarah, I had this experience I want to tell you about. It was a dream. Actually, I don't really know if it was a regular kind of dream. It was different from anything I have ever experienced. My father came to me as a teacher," I began.

Sarah looked at me intently.

"It was like I was in the presence of pure love," I continued. "He told me that all kinds of love—for a friend, a child, an animal, a place, a lover—are all the same thing. He also said that love is all that matters and he urged me to appreciate it in all its forms. Then he said, and he was chuckling when he said this, that the earth from the heavens looks just like the heavens from the earth. From the heavens the earth looks like a zillion stars. The stars are the love that humans are truly experiencing in their lives. After he said that, I woke up."

"Wow," Sarah said softly. "I'm glad you told me. Thank you. Could I tell Hillary about the dream? I think it would help her."

"Of course," I replied.

We talked for awhile about people and events back home. Then the phone rang. It was Patton calling to see how Sarah was and to find out how long I planned to stay. "Missing your roomy, are you?" she said to Patton, smiling at me, eyebrows raised.

I stuck my tongue out at her and smirked in response, my lighthearted facial expression belying the hard knot that had formed in my gut. I wanted badly to talk seriously with Sarah about this scheme she had to set me up with her husband if she died. I ached for the words to come tumbling out of my mouth but none did.

I arrived back at the apartment in time to help Patton put the girls to bed. Bedtime had become an overly long ritual with many last minute requests and reluctance to fall asleep, reflecting the stress they were experiencing.

After the girls fell asleep, Patton and I sat on the couch and began to talk. He told me about the mix of feelings he had experienced during Sarah's illness. Much to his and Sarah's surprise, they now both recognized that Sarah's illness contained many gifts for their relationship and for each of them individually. Patton said that he never would have thought that life could feel good in the midst of the constant wearing demands and the potential loss that was never far from consciousness. At some point in the process, he and Sarah had found peace with not needing to side with one outcome or the other. They would fight with every available resource for Sarah to live, but they would not define themselves by the outcome. It was a peaceful surrender to a greater will.

I told Patton about the dream with my father and that I had also shared it with Sarah. Patton listened intently and, with no hesitation, accepted the experience as being real and important. When we eventually looked at our watches, we could not believe how late it was. 3 A.M.!

Neither of us had stayed up that late talking for years. I went to bed once again filled to overflowing with the intensity of feeling that all our lives had crossed for a reason.

Over the next three days I visited Sarah often. I found myself eager to be at the hospital. I would experience the remarkable inner stillness as soon as I walked through the elevator doors to Sarah's floor. Sarah and I would talk about whatever came to either of us. Conversation floated freely from the impact of television on children, to the frustrations of not knowing whether one would live or die during the next months, to shared silence.

In between visits to the hospital, I helped with the chores that were difficult to do without an extra helping hand. Hillary and I went on an adventure to get her hair cut. Ivana and I went shopping for a new pair of walking shoes for Sarah. I went grocery and vitamin shopping, filling a small bag with the variety of vitamins and minerals the whole family was taking to try to keep their immune systems strong so that no one would become ill and pass the illness to Sarah, whose immune system was barely functioning.

During the three days I spent in Seattle, I felt aware of every moment. Life felt dense and rich and connected.

—12—

After final embraces and promises to return as soon as possible, I pulled away from the apartment building to go home. I was grateful for the hours of silent driving ahead. After finding the highway and settling into the monotony of driving, I allowed myself, with an internal sigh of relief, to become absorbed in the experiences of the last few days.

As I lost myself in thought, the "knowing" that Sarah would die seemed to open in front of me like an ocean. There it was. I gazed at its expansiveness. I listened to its steadiness. It was truth. I sank quietly into its depths. There, suspended in the stillness of Sarah's death, the truth of my own dying emerged silently, gently rolling and swaying in the invisible currents of these depths. I drifted, watching this truth, imagining myself with a terminal illness. I saw myself dead, my body still and empty. For the first time I could remember, I did not push the thought of my own death away. As if in exchange for the tremendous energy usually expended on keeping death at a safe distance, I relaxed into an expansive freedom I had never known. I felt unshackled from all the fears, small and large, that had always been present in my life. It was as if facing this ultimate fear unlocked the door which held all other fears, releasing the captured energy to merge instantly with the greater Whole. Fear seemed an illusion, a mirage I could no longer even find.

Then I sank further and found the truth of my children's deaths. The possibility that I could experience the loss of my children had always been a thought I could barely hold, even momentarily, before rejecting it with every ounce of strength I had. Living with this potential loss had been the one real downside I could identify with having children. Now, in amazement, I found myself floating easily in the midst of this thought. I knew that I would experience intense pain if they were to die before me, but death no longer seemed the enemy I had always thought it was. I understood that each of their deaths are theirs, connected wholly to each of their lives.

Then the experience in the parking lot, months earlier, after Sarah had "planted the kernel" of Patton and me being in a relationship if she died, floated in front of me. I remembered the tremendous internal conflict, "the crash," I had experienced when I realized that I had associated Sarah's death with euphoria. The reality of Sarah's death and the euphoria I had experienced no longer seemed opposed. The boundaries between what had appeared to be opposites had disappeared. I seemed to be floating between the two sides, where opposites meet and things simply are what they are.

I looked around in this boundless place and was filled with joy. I saw that nothing separated anything from anything else. *Where is the boundary between nothing and everything?* I mused. *Even these opposites do not exist. They are the same. Who I really am is this nothing which is everything!* This paradox was immensely humorous to me. The swell of laughter rumbled in my gut like claps of thunder. At the heart of the joke was the realization that the "rules" of this awareness were different from the "rules" of logical, rational thinking. To try to understand from a place of logic that "nothing" and "everything" are really the same seemed absurd, and yet this insight was far more meaningful than anything I had ever deduced using the rules of the intellect. I realized I needed to see beyond the intellect to understand what was most important.

Then my mind went back in time to sitting in my car in the hospital parking lot. I remembered how I had felt that the whole universe had somehow shifted and had aligned itself perfectly. I grinned at the memory, realizing that, like a child inside a moving car watching the moon "follow me," the universe had not moved at all—I had.

This was a level of awareness that seemed truer than anything I had ever known. In this place where human illusion dissolves, what is left is good and loving and all-embracing. I stared and stared at this truth, unable to shift focus, it seemed so remarkable and wonderful to me. I felt connected to the bits of all religions that I had ever had contact with and with the billions of people throughout the world and throughout the ages who had experienced the peaceful centeredness that comes from connecting to a loving source.

I was very surprised when the image of Jesus on the cross floated through my thoughts. With a start, I felt like I found the answer to a question I had never been able to understand: how Jesus was able to forgive and indeed embrace his executioners. The answer was that he had lived in this remarkable place! He had lived here, between opposites, where everything is connected and human illusion dissolves. To Jesus, love and hate were not opposites! The illusions that drive human lives must have been painfully apparent to him. For the first time in my life, I was filled with love for this remarkable man who had changed history with his message of compassion and inclusion.

Then the dream experience with my father came to the forefront of my thoughts. I smiled, remembering the dream and feeling like I was ready and eager to understand better the meaning of the dream.

Lives are unnecessarily bound by untruths of our own making, I said to myself, remembering what my father had said.

Yes, I thought, *maybe he meant that we create boundaries between things that are really the same; we even create opposites from wholes.*

Earth from the heavens looks like the heavens from earth. What you see of earth from the heavens are millions of tiny starlike lights, I continued. *Heaven and earth are mirror images. They are the same? Life and death are the same?* I asked myself. *They are opposites like love and hate. Is this too an illusion? Is there a place in-between these opposites where they are the same?*

As I struggled with understanding how life and death could be the same, the feeling of peace and centeredness began to lessen, replaced by a much more familiar sense of effort and guardedness. I did not want to lose the peace I had so recently found, so I decided just to let the interpretation of the dream be. As soon as I let go of trying to understand the dream, I was totally in the present and could let things "be as they are." I wanted to stay in that place forever.

It was not until I arrived home that I understood fully the impact of what I had experienced on the drive home. At home I was surrounded by what was most familiar to me. Nothing on the exterior had changed. My kids were hungry for dinner. I needed to go over my lecture for tomorrow's class. There were phone messages to return and mail to open. Yet, what I experienced on the inside was different than anything I had ever felt. Love radiated from me as if a window had been swung wide open. The love was not connected to any circumstance or event; it came from a source within. It was the purest joy I had ever known.

I tried to relate the feeling to anything I had experienced before but I couldn't. Being in love was the best, the most expansive and grandest emotion I had ever had. But this was not exactly like being in love, even a thousand times over. It was more like being free, absolutely free. And clear. So clear it was as if one could look through this love for millions and millions of miles and nothing, not even a speck, would obstruct the view.

I experienced this awareness for about two days, and then my fear that it would not last seemed to consume it. Now I believe that I opened for a short time to who I really am, who we all really are beyond our fears and defenses. I continue to marvel at the fact that what seemed to open the gate to this place was simply being with what is. Until we are able to be still with the truth of the brevity and fragility of our earthly existence, we will defend ourselves from who we really are and the limitless love that is our potential.

—13—

"Patton and I were wondering if you might be able to help us out," Sarah said after calling and saying hello.

"Of course. What's up?" I asked, anxious to hear.

"They're letting me come home."

"Oh, wow! When?" I exclaimed.

"Well, it's still tentative but in a couple of weeks. The problem is, I can't drive yet. We could rent a truck and pull the car but then there wouldn't be room for all of us in the truck. Do you think you could rent a truck down there and drive it up? You could either drive the truck or the car back down and Patton could drive the other vehicle. Maybe Hillary or Ivana could drive with you. Ha, you'd probably end up with both of them. They like you a lot."

"That would be fine with me. I like them too. I definitely want to help you move back. It would give me a feeling of closure since I helped you guys move up there."

"I'm sure we could get someone else to help but you are Patton's and my first choice," Sarah said sincerely.

"Gee, Sarah, I'm honored."

After we hung up, I stared into space, my hand still on the receiver. I wanted badly to feel hopeful and happy, to think about things that I could do with Sarah and Patton when they returned, but instead I felt like crying.

"Damnit, maybe you are wrong!" I said to the part of me that doubted Sarah's return.

That part was not in the least affected by my anger. It seemed to reply, "It just is."

I felt cornered. On the one hand, I wanted desperately for the "knowing" part of me to be wrong about Sarah's impending death. On the other hand, the idea that the "knowing" was false was also frightening. If I was wrong about this, I was not sure what I could trust. Then I found my new mantra, "What is, is. What is, is," I repeated and quickly calmed.

Instead of thinking through the details of making the trip in a couple of weeks, I busied myself with other things. I never made plans to go.

A week before Sarah, Patton and the girls were to return to Corvallis, ninety-two days after the bone marrow transplant, Sarah called and left a message on my answering machine. "I've got some pretty bad news. I need to talk with you as soon as possible. We are not going to be returning to Corvallis when we thought. Please give me a call."

I heard the message and my insides froze. *I don't want to be right about this!* I screamed internally.

Linda was with me when I hung up the phone. "What's wrong?" she asked looking at my sullen expression.

"The leukemia's back."

"Oh no! That's what she said?"

"No, but it's back."

"Let me hear the message."

"Go ahead."

Linda listened to the message and said, "Maybe it's not so bad. Sarah doesn't sound too upset."

Nothing could have shaken my conviction that the reason they were not coming back as planned was because the leukemia had returned.

"Why do you think the leukemia is back?" Linda queried.

I wanted to say, "Because for some God-knows-what-reason I am tapped into knowing what's going to happen. I know it like I know that you are Linda or that I am standing here. I just know."

Instead I said, "Sarah always sounds that way when things are really bad and besides, she would have just told me in the message if it wasn't serious."

"I think you are right but I don't want to think you are right," Linda admitted.

I called back and Sarah answered. "Looks like plans have changed. They found leukemia, ten percent."

"Oh no, Sarah."

Sarah was silent and then said, "Yeah, it's not very good news. I asked for a biopsy before we left. My tooth ached and my glands were swollen in my groin. Those symptoms have always been right.

"There are still things they can do," she continued. "Actually, we got some really good news. There's a brand new experimental treatment. It shows promise. There are other possibilities too. I don't want to talk about it any more now though."

"Sarah, I'm sorry," I said, emotion seeping through my words.

"Could you come up for a visit sometime?" Sarah asked.

"Yes, I want to. I miss you guys."

—14—

I was in a grocery store walking down an aisle when I found myself, once again, in touch with my internal landscape. In a startled instant I saw that it was no longer a desert. Instead, it was alive with growth. I peered around, trying to understand what had replaced the desert. Suddenly I saw. It was me.

My breath came short and my spine tingled at the discovery. Then I panicked as I realized that this "me" that was growing was different from the "me" I was used to relating to. This new "me" was not my internalization of what others said I was. It was not the me of my family or friends, or colleagues, or society. At the moment of this realization, I felt a loss as profound as any I have ever experienced. It was like watching a sudden, horrible accident that I was helpless to change.

Then, as if running to the scene of the accident, not knowing what I would find, I began to take toll of the damage. In a moment's flash, I understood that being in love would never feel the same. "I will never fall head-over-heels in love knowing that the person is perfect and will make me happy. I will never believe that I could be happy if only someone would say or do the right thing to make me happy."

I was terrified at this discovery. How was I to live without the hope that someone else could make my life right and good and happy? I did not want to be bottom line in charge of me. I was not ready for this responsibility. Not yet. Not until I had more time to sort through things.

This new place seemed dull and serious and devastatingly real without escape. Even the desert was better than this. How could life have left me here?

Then I noticed Death was present everywhere in the landscape; it was the dirt from which everything else was growing. "We die alone. We die alone. There will come a time when your life is only yours," it seemed to pulse

Through my immediate terror, I had the barest glimmer of understanding that the growth that had emerged from the desert could be good and not something to fear. After all, life had changed a lot over the last months and, as difficult as the changes had been, I did not regret them. I breathed deeply.

All of this happened as I walked down the aisle, automatically taking the usual groceries off the shelves and placing them in the cart. I was in two entirely different places at the same time. Suddenly, a story my father had told me about being in two places at the same time appeared in my thoughts. One of the steps in his fight against colon cancer had been a colostomy. After the operation, when he had returned to work, he told me about sitting in a meeting with fellow university administrators and having a bowel movement right there in the meeting. "No one had a clue!" he had laughed aloud. I had joined him in hearty laughter. "Good one, Dad!"

15

Sarah became only the second person in the world to receive the new treatment. The protocol was to test the drug for safety, not for effectiveness. She would receive a dose that was a fraction of what the doctors thought would actually reduce the leukemia. Sarah decided to undergo the treatment, in part because it was her best chance in a drastically reduced arena of chances, and in part because she had a strong desire to contribute to scientific efforts to find an effective treatment for this disease.

Much to everyone's amazement, the first dose of the drug cut the leukemia in half. The research team was thrilled. Sarah wanted to keep even and not be taken for a ride, but she also expressed hope.

I arranged to visit the following week. My older son, Zach, had an ice hockey tournament in the area and my mother and my mother's sister, who was visiting from Tennessee, were going to come down and see part of the tournament. After the tournament, the plan was for everyone to spend one night at my cousin's home in Seattle. After that, my mother and aunt would drive north to Vancouver. I would drive half way home with my children and meet Linda who would drive them the rest of the way. I would turn around and head back up to Seattle for a three day visit with Sarah, Patton and the girls.

The day after the tournament ended, my mother, my aunt, my two sons, and my cousin met Patton, Sarah, Hillary and Ivana in a Seattle park.

Sarah greeted me with a big hug saying, "I'd better hug you now since my counts are up and I'm not sure how long that will last."

It was wonderful seeing Sarah out of the hospital, walking around, being with her family. Sarah, my mother, and my aunt sat on a bench watching the children and talking. I was occupied with the children and ventured over to the bench to chat when I could. My mother was trying to interact, but it seemed very difficult for her to follow the conversation. I wondered whether her hearing had continued to deteriorate. I had told Sarah that my mother was an outgoing, social person and was a bit disappointed that she could not converse easily with Sarah.

That night my mother, aunt, two sons and I spent the night at my cousin's home. At two thirty in the morning, my younger son, Corey, woke up screaming in pain from what we called growing pains. I carried him downstairs and put ice on his leg, rubbed his back, and gave him some Tylenol. He fell asleep on the couch and I carried him back to bed. Within half an hour he was screaming again. I carried him downstairs and, after trying everything I could think of, decided to drive him around in the car to see if that would help. I wrapped him in a blanket and carried him to the car. Within fifteen minutes he was sound asleep. We returned to the house and he slept the rest of the night. I, however, could not get back to sleep.

When we left the next morning, I felt overcome with exhaustion. The exhaustion left me defenseless against the utter sadness I felt about Sarah's leukemia returning. When we arrived at the meeting place, a loud pizza parlor, I could not imagine turning around and going back up to Seattle. I knew that I would not be able to be anything but real, and real was sad and tired and overcome with all the feelings of the last year. Despite the deep conversations I had enjoyed with Sarah and Patton, I had never expressed openly and fully all of the pain I felt about Sarah's illness, nor the full extent of how Sarah's illness had impacted me. I was hesitant to express my pain, and I was petrified that I would not be able to hide it in my present state.

I called Sarah and Patton to let them know I would not be returning to Seattle. No one answered, so I left a message saying that I was totally tired and was going home. I arrived home to a message from Sarah. She sounded more distressed than I had ever heard her. The message said that she and Patton were very disappointed that I was not coming and were worried that they had offended me. I broke down with the phone still in my hand. Then I went outside and sat on a bench by the side of my house and cried tears of exhaustion, sadness, and bewilderment at the occurrences of the last months. I would contain my tears for a few moments only to be heaving with sobs the next. After I had finally let go and cried until the jerks and sobs had stopped, I found myself drained of all but what was real in the moment.

I called Sarah and immediately told her what I was feeling. "Sarah, I feel so sad and tired right now I just couldn't make the trip to Seattle."

"Patton and I are afraid that we did something to offend you," Sarah replied with a serious, worried tone.

"Oh God no, Sarah! It's nothing like that. I feel so sad that the leukemia is back and I didn't know if it would be okay to be sad. You know, we've never really been sad together and that's all I feel right now. I didn't think I would be able to defend myself against this sadness and I was afraid it would be bad for you all. I didn't want you to be in a position of taking care of me," I said crying openly.

"You and Patton could have cried together, he's having a pretty rough time," she replied. "I really wish you had come. I am not saying this to make you feel guilty but I feel very lonely," she said slowly, as if the words were a burden not only to feel but also to express.

"I am so sorry, Sarah. I just didn't think I could make it up there. I would do anything to be able to be there right now."

"I wish you could be too," Sarah stated sadly. "Patton would like to talk to you too."

I said the same things to Patton I had said to Sarah. He told me he understood and hoped that I would visit soon.

I hung up the phone feeling intensely connected to both of them. It was as if the story that was unfolding had reached the end of one chapter and had begun another. I immediately turned my attention to arranging a visit the following week.

16

I arrived in Seattle the evening before Sarah was to receive the second dose of the new treatment. I drove to the apartment building and circled numerous times trying to find a parking space. A few blocks from the building I finally succeeded. I walked to the front entrance and pressed the intercom. Patton answered.

"Welcome. Come on up. We're just getting dinner ready," he said.

I took the familiar elevator and knocked on their apartment door. No one answered. I knocked a little louder and someone opened the door but, when I took a step inside, no one greeted me and I couldn't tell who had opened the door. Patton and Sarah were working in the kitchen and Ivana was sitting on the living room floor playing. I was momentarily taken aback by the silence and wondered whether I should have come.

Then Sarah said, "Welcome, we're glad you are here," as if reading my thoughts.

Patton echoed Sarah's greeting as I walked to the couch and sat.

"Ivana, did you see that Pat's here?" Sarah prodded.

Ivana looked up, said "Hi", then put her head down again, absorbed in her play.

"Where's Hillary?" I asked.

"In her room playing," Sarah replied.

I sat on the couch in silence as everyone continued to do what they had been doing before I arrived. I had grown used to feeling like an insider and now I felt like an outsider. I discovered as I sat that I was a calm outsider, peaceful in my silent observation.

Then Sarah called everyone to dinner. Hillary came out of her room and greeted me enthusiastically. I gave her a big hug before sitting down at the dinner table. After everyone was served, we all relaxed into being with each other. The children ate quickly and left to play.

After dinner, Patton, Sarah, and I sat around the table and talked. The topic was fear. Sarah said she had recently experienced two days of intense fear of dying. She described the physical sensation of terror, how it had gripped her so tightly she could barely function. Now that she was through that period, she felt different.

"It doesn't have such a hold on me and I doubt it ever will again," she said.

I told Sarah that my understanding of fear had changed over the last few months, that I had become aware of the tremendous role that fear plays in people's lives.

"I had no idea how much fear directs my life," I said. "I had a few hours of not being enslaved by fear, and now I see fear everywhere in my life and in other people's lives. It's like we define things in a certain way, based on our experiences. Anything that falls outside of those boundaries we fear. But it's all an illusion—we created the boundaries in the first place! And you know, what's right there on the other side of fear is love. It's so amazing, love just sits there and we fence it off with all this fear."

Sarah smiled. "Yeah, I think you're right. You know I had so much fear at the beginning of this illness, when I was diagnosed."

She then told me she had been writing the story of her illness and that she would like me to read what she had written so far. I told her I would be honored, and she handed me the pages she had written. I cleaned up the dinner dishes, said good-night, and left for the studio apartment one floor down where I was staying.

After getting into bed, I eagerly started to read what Sarah had written. She began by describing the strain of beginning graduate school, how little time there had been those first months in school for things she had always enjoyed. Then she was at the Health Service getting blood work done.

> *While the doctor was examining me I asked her casually if she thought it could be cancer. That hadn't really been a concern. She seemed to think it wasn't and said it could be mono, although this would be unusual at my age. She wanted me to get some blood work done. I went to the lab, had the blood drawn and waited in the hallway until the lab technician handed me the results. While I was waiting I heard someone in the lab say, 'Oh no!'*

As I continued to read I became privy to the part of the story I had missed, the months after Sarah's diagnosis when I had felt unable to contact her. I read with fascination her initial reaction to being told she had cancer.

> *My body felt paralyzed with fear. My head whirled and my thoughts spun. Cancer, some form of what? What do you mean*

cancer? We were talking mono, not cancer. What have I done wrong? How will my children live without me? The youngest wouldn't even remember me. I know . . . My dad died when I was only seven and I haven't many memories of him. Seven. That's the age of my oldest. Oh God!

. . . The next thing I remember is my husband and me lying next to each other crying. The fear was intolerable. The pain and agony at the thought of having to leave my children was more than I could bear. I didn't let myself go so deep into the feeling for fear I could not return. I thought of the adage that God gives you only as much as you can handle. I didn't believe it at that moment. How could a God let a mother suffer so in the thought of having to say goodbye to her children? At age almost four and seven they needed me and I them. I wasn't finished. I wanted to see them grow up and become their own individuals. I wanted to see what direction life would encourage them into, to be there if they had babies themselves. I wasn't ready to die yet and the last thing I wanted for them was to share my lonely fate after the death of my father.

. . . The biopsy shows you have a form of leukemia called AML or Acute Nonlymphocitic Leukemia. He kept talking. I couldn't take it in. I was hoping my husband was listening. Leukemia. That was the only one the Health Center doctor had not mentioned and all the other diagnoses felt like a dream to me. But this one. It resonated. Yes, I had leukemia and on some level I knew it and accepted it. I started asking questions and he patiently answered them all. I could not stay in my intellect for very long and started to sob. What about our children? My husband moved his chair closer to me and the doctor caringly touched my hand again. How did I get this? What did I do? He tried to reassure me it was not something I had done, that the origins of leukemia are seldom known . . .

How long we were in his office was unclear, maybe one or two hours. It was Saturday morning and he said I wouldn't have to enter the hospital until Monday unless I got a fever. He had clearly explained the options, and the plan was two phases of chemotherapy and then a bone marrow transplant. This would give me my best chances for survival. We would have to tell the children today, just in case I developed a fever which did in fact begin by early evening.

I can't describe the agony I felt in having to say goodbye to my children that night. We called our youngest child's home daycare person and asked if she could help. She was more than willing and I was grateful. We'd only lived in this town six months, so we hadn't many close friends and no relatives. My husband could take me to the hospital, and I knew the children were with someone they knew and cared about. When my then seven year old started to cry and say she was scared I wouldn't come back, that I would die, the intergenerational similarities to the death of my father took me by complete surprise. I had been told he had a plane crash but not that he had died. I knew he was dead even though all the adults denied it. This was how it was done in the fifties. So when my daughter asked, I couldn't deny to her that this illness could be fatal, but I emphasized I had every intention of surviving and I would do everything I could to make that happen. "But I'm afraid!" she cried. So was I. I had a twenty-five to thirty-five percent chance of making it, depending on which treatment I chose. The odds were not in my favor. I wasn't going to lie to her as I had been lied to . . .

I assured her that her daddy would be back as soon as he could and they would both come see me in the hospital tomorrow. I had to go. I was concerned about my rising temperature. The separation from her was unnatural. We belonged together and we were being torn apart by something we had no control over. But she didn't see it that way, and she let me know that when I finally returned home thirty-three days later. My reception home was her rage at me for not having given her enough time to say goodbye. She had let this build over the month and never said a word about it to me even though she visited me daily during that month. I held her and let her cry and scream it out, sometimes trying to rationalize the situation, but that was not what she needed. This time I did my best to give her what I thought she needed, to be very present with her and let her express herself. Although very challenging for me, I hoped this was what she needed. We held each other for a long time . . .

Her writing stopped at this point. I lay in bed and stared ahead, remembering the tremendous conflicting emotions I had experienced during the months Sarah had written about. She had been almost a stranger then, and yet I had felt intensely connected to what I imagined she was experiencing. Now, for the first time, I knew that what I had imagined was true. For a few moments I was filled with a surge of the compelling energy that had entered my life so abruptly after I learned of Sarah's diagnosis. "Sarah," I whispered, "what brought our lives together like this?"

Then my thoughts turned to the remarkable changes that had occurred in Sarah. She had moved from this level of fear to a kind of faith that, while she certainly hoped to continue living, whatever happened would simply be. How had this transformation occurred?

I found myself thinking about all of the conversations I had enjoyed with Sarah and those unwaveringly honest eyes. She always wanted to know the truth from me whether it was about kids, work, my personal struggles, or dying. I would find myself locked in her gaze, returning her intensity. I had never been able to be anything but authentic, who I really was at the moment, with Sarah. Being with Sarah, I had learned about stillness; we simply were.

This is how I envisioned Sarah's relationship with death. At the beginning, after her diagnosis, she did not want to relate to death, it was too frightening. But once she was ready, she engaged death in an intense conversation. She opened herself to receiving truth. Remarkably, even in the face of dying, she did not ask for wellness, nor even happiness, only truth. Through this process she learned to be present with death, to understand that it simply was. I fell asleep feeling a comradeship with death, both of us having been the target of that intense, honest stare.

Sarah and Patton had to leave for the hospital early the next morning. The plan was for me to get the girls ready for school and day care. When I arrived early in the morning, the girls were still in bed and Sarah and Patton were ready to leave for the hospital. As soon as they left, Hillary was out of bed getting dressed, then sitting on the couch as I ate a bowl of cereal at the nearby kitchen table.

"I don't think it's my mom's time to die but if it is, I want you to be my mom," she said smiling at me.

I froze. Think fast! I panicked, trying to swallow the spoonful of cereal I had just put in my mouth. "You know Hillary," I managed to say calmly, "it's hard to know what will happen in life, but I can tell you that I care very much about you and your sister and your mom and dad. No matter what happens, we will be friends."

"Okay," Hillary shrugged.

"Then Zach and Corey would be my brothers," she ventured shyly.

I gave her a hug. "Yep, I guess that would be true, huh?" She hugged me back.

As is true of eight year olds, the subject quickly changed and we became engrossed in trying to make a dress for one of her dolls. At eight forty-five Hillary caught the van to the school for children who had parents or siblings being treated at Fred Hutchinson and Julie, Ivana's day care provider, arrived to pick up Ivana.

I walked the few blocks to the hospital full of tension about what to say to Sarah and Patton about my conversation with Hillary. I was reaching the end of my ability to deal with such life changing matters without involving those whose lives would change with mine.

My conflict was readily resolved by Sarah who, before I could sit, asked me how it had gone with the kids. I replied that the girls had gotten off just fine. This obviously was not what she really wanted to know. Had I talked with the girls? What had they said? Was the conversation meaningful? With Patton sitting in a chair across from me, on the opposite side of Sarah's bed, I took a deep breath and, feeling like I was stepping off a high diving board, told them what Hillary had said.

They looked at each other and Patton said, "So she said this directly to you? Yes, we have been hearing this too. What did you say to her?"

"I said, no matter what happens I want us to be friends."

Patton said he thought this was a good reply. Sarah told me how much she thought it comforted Hillary to think that I would be there if she died. Besides, Hillary would love to have a couple of brothers. She chuckled at this and looked at Patton who smiled back. Then, with a glint in her eye, she looked at me and then at Patton and said, "I bet this makes you two feel comfortable!" I looked down, too overwhelmed to look directly at either Sarah or Patton.

The nurse entered the room and, much to my relief, the conversation shifted focus quickly. The treatment had not yet begun because Sarah's blood counts were extremely low and the nurse had some anxiety about starting the treatment without approval from the doctor. The nurse told us that the head of the research team would be in soon. The world famous researcher arrived a half an hour later and used a dry ink board in the room to illustrate possible reasons that Sarah's counts were so low. Patton and Sarah asked insightful questions based on the considerable knowledge of this disease they had accumulated over the last thirteen months.

After answering all of Sarah and Patton's questions, the doctor gave his approval to begin the treatment. It was now approaching lunch time. I suggested that Patton and I take turns going for lunch so that one of us could keep Sarah company. Sarah responded quite definitely that the nurse had to be with her at all times during the treatment, and she rather liked the nurse so it would be better for me and Patton to go ahead and have lunch together. I sighed and Sarah smiled.

At lunch, Patton asked me how being in this position felt to me. I replied that I felt like going for a long walk to try to figure it all out.

"Yeah," he said meeting my eyes with genuine empathy.

"How about you, Patton?" I asked. "How does it feel to have your wife pick out a replacement for herself?"

"Well, I think she's made a good choice," he said.

Sarah spent that night in the hospital because she developed a fever, an expected side effect of the treatment. Patton stayed for a while at the hospital with Sarah and I tried to put the children to bed. Going to sleep was hard without a good-night from their dad. Ivana snuggled with me on the couch and was drifting off to sleep when her father arrived. After Patton said good-night, both girls fell asleep. Patton and I agreed that we had better not even start a conversation because we could lose track of time again.

Sarah had a bone marrow biopsy scheduled for the next morning at ten thirty. The plan was for me to help get Hillary off to school and then spend an hour with Ivana before Julie, her baby sitter, arrived. I would then go to the hospital to be with Sarah and Patton during the biopsy.

After Hillary left, I took a shower and got changed. As I sat on the couch in the living room putting on my socks, Ivana noticed a small hole in one of them. Since I was wearing sandals, she thought I should be concerned and suggested I sew up the hole. I told her I would but I didn't know if they had a needle and thread. She jumped up, dragged a chair to the refrigerator and, before I could say a word, retrieved a sewing kit from the top of the refrigerator. Then she sat down next to me, opened the kit and started to look for the right color thread to mend my sock.

"My mommy can't sew because she has cancer," she stated, still rummaging through the sewing kit.

"Oh really, why not?" I asked, thinking that perhaps it could be dangerous because she could prick herself.

"The cancer could get on the thread and then other people could get it," Ivana stated matter-of-factly.

My easy enjoyment of sharing the morning with Ivana suddenly turned serious. I looked squarely at Ivana, giving her my full attention and hoping she would give me her full attention.

"Ivana, do you think that a person with cancer can give it to someone else?" I asked, anxious for her reply.

She put the sewing kit down, stood up with her hands on her hips, furrowed her eyebrows and stated, "Cancer spreads. The doctor told *me*," as if she couldn't believe that I, a grown-up, could be so stupid.

"Ivana, the doctor meant that the cancer inside of your mom can spread from one part of her body to another part. But your mom could never ever give you or your sister or your daddy or anyone else cancer. Really, I know I am right about this."

She listened to me very intently, breath and heart rate slowed, eyes directly focused on mine. Then she sat, picked up the sewing kit, and resumed her search for the correct color thread. She chose a thread and handed it to me. Following her instructions, I put a few stitches in my sock. Then I put the sock on my foot and declared the project a success. Ivana was very happy that my sock had been repaired, and I was glad to share an experience of making something better with this preschooler who was learning far too early that not everything can be fixed.

The rest of our time together was spent with Ivana in my lap, holding my neck with one hand, her gesture of security, and playing with my earrings and necklace with her other hand. At the end of our hour the phone rang. Ivana ran to get it. It was Julie.

"Excuse me, but you are interrupting our conversation," Ivana said to Julie and then handed the phone to me. Julie and I laughed and then agreed to meet downstairs in a few minutes.

After saying goodbye to Ivana and Julie, I walked to the hospital and tried to figure out why Sarah wanted me to be present for her bone marrow biopsy. She had made it very clear that she wanted me there by asking me repeatedly if I wanted to be there. She had told me this was an opportunity she was certain I would not want to miss, something I would probably never see again. As I walked towards the hospital, I felt as if I was traveling through a tunnel leading me to a more intimate relationship with Sarah and with her illness. I welcomed closeness to Sarah but was scared of the reality of her cancer.

I found Sarah in a bed in the outpatient clinic with Patton by her side. I pulled up a chair. Sarah was in an upbeat mood and cheerfully asked how things had gone with Ivana. I told them what Ivana had said about cancer spreading. They were concerned and agreed with each other to talk to Ivana about the fact that she was in no danger of getting cancer from her mother. The nurse soon arrived to tell Sarah they were ready for her.

We walked to a room that reminded me of the emergency department of the hospital back home that I had visited a few times for my children's various mishaps. The walls were lined with shelves stocked with supplies, and there was a bed in the middle of the room allowing access to the patient on all sides.

After consulting with Sarah about pain medications, a nurse gave her Demerol through her IV. A few minutes later, a team of three medical personnel entered the room with a cart carrying various instruments and containers. Two of the three were wearing odd tinted glasses that made them look ready for the beach. The third member of the team, a nurse, asked Sarah if she was ready. Sarah replied, in a slightly groggy voice, that she thought she was ready. The nurse pulled down Sarah's pants to expose her right hip and then prepared the area. As this was happening, I was sitting in a chair close to the bed. Sarah's head was turned in my direction. We looked at each other. My hand went to my heart and Sarah smiled, closed mouth.

The nurse said, "We're ready to go."

Patton was holding Sarah's hand. He suggested that I rub Sarah's leg because it seemed to help the pain. I stood up and hesitantly put my hands on the back of Sarah's right leg. The long needle was inserted and then the nurse pushed and twisted it into Sarah's hip. This part of the procedure seemed to be relatively painless for Sarah. Patton explained that the painful part was pulling out the bone marrow.

The nurse said, "Okay Sarah, here we go. Take a deep breath and let it out." As Sarah was exhaling, the nurse pulled up on the syringe and the red marrow entered the tube. Sarah groaned and grimaced as the syringe filled. I rubbed her leg the best I could, wishing I knew better what would help. After the first draw, the nurse handed the marrow to the other two clinicians. They spread a small amount of the marrow between two clear petri dishes and examined it closely, looking for granules. Another draw was needed they said quickly and to the point. My heart sank as the nurse began the procedure again. Not again! At least apologize to Sarah or acknowledge how hard this must be for Sarah to have to go through again. What about Sarah's feelings and pain in this? My heart pounded as the needle was once again inserted. What if this one isn't good either? I wasn't sure I could stand this one more time.

The second draw was successful. Sarah was given a few minutes to rest and then was helped off the bed. She stood unsteadily.

"Sarah, take an arm so you don't fall," I said with more emotion than I meant to reveal. Sarah placed her hand in the crook of Patton's arm and took a few steps. I shifted Sarah's bag that I had picked up to my outside arm and offered my free arm to Sarah. The three of us walked slowly down the hall to the waiting room. We found seats together with Sarah sitting in the middle. Patton got up to do something and Sarah turned groggily to me.

"So, what did you think?" she asked slowly but with genuine interest in my reaction.

I debated for a moment how honest to be. Total honesty won. "I hated how intrusive it was, Sarah. I hated that they invade your very bone," I said emotionally.

She looked at me evenly and seriously and simply said, "Yes."

A nurse came out of a small room and told Sarah she could come in. I was surprised by this; I wasn't sure what we had been waiting for. I found myself sitting alone and I began to look around the waiting area. There were ten to fifteen patients sitting or coming or going. The patients were easily identified by their scarves or their baldness, their hospital attire, or, in some cases, their bloated faces.

Panic caught fire in my gut. These people were everyone. They were old, young, men, women, fat, thin, attractive, ugly. This could happen to anyone. This could happen to me or, Oh God!, to one of my kids. Life suddenly felt unbearably unpredictable. My head throbbed with the fear of an unordered, chaotic, and meaningless world.

Patton returned and sat down next to me. "Sarah's getting her blood work done. It doesn't take long," he said calmly. "How are you doing?"

His words jolted me away from my fear as suddenly as I had entered it. "I'm fine, thanks. The medical part of the biopsy didn't bother me but I really hated how intrusive it is. They dig right into her bones."

Just then Sarah walked from the small room towards us. Patton and

I both stood. Sarah motioned to us to stay seated. "We have to wait a few minutes," she said.

She sat down next to me and, once again, asked me what I thought of the biopsy.

"It's pretty intense," I said.

"Yes," she said and closed her eyes.

We left a few minutes later, Sarah's right arm interlocked with Patton's and her left arm interlocked with mine, as we walked slowly toward the elevator. I will remember this moment, I thought. The three of us together. It seemed exactly as it should be.

17

I had been planning for a couple of weeks to go up to Seattle on Thursday, June fifteenth for a three day visit. This was going to be my fifth visit to Seattle. Except for the details at home that had to be taken care of before traveling, the trip to Seattle now felt comfortable and familiar.

The new experimental treatment had reduced but not eliminated the leukemia. Unless the leukemia could be completely eradicated, it would increase rapidly and Sarah would die. Treatment options had become very limited.

Patton called a week before I was to leave with news that the latest test results showed the leukemia had escalated dramatically. The only ray of hope was chemotherapy. Chemotherapy, however, had a good chance of shortening Sarah's life and little chance of prolonging it for very long. I decided not to wait until Thursday and to go up on Tuesday after a morning work meeting. Sarah's condition continued to worsen over the week-end and Linda and Leslie decided to go up to Seattle on Tuesday as well.

I awoke Tuesday morning, June thirteenth, with a calm, introverted focus. I looked at my watch. It was nine minutes after seven, just when I needed to get up. Then I noticed the second hand was not moving; the watch had stopped. This seemed very strange. It had never once stopped in all the years I had used it. I tried winding it and tapping the crystal but it would not go. I was filled with the combination of low level anxiety and cautious wonder that had become familiar to me over the last year.

My first thought was that the watch stopping was a sign that Sarah had already died. This did not seem right though, not yet. I checked the time on another clock. It said seven fifteen. My watch had stopped just minutes earlier. The two sides of me that had struggled many times the last year took up arms. The logic side said this was a coincidence, watches eventually break and stop. The intuitive side, however, insisted there was some meaning to my watch stopping that morning at that time.

Without resolving my internal battle, I got up and went through the motions of getting myself showered and ready to go and getting the kids ready for school. Most of my energy was engaged internally. Thirteen years ago on this day my father had died. It seemed so odd that I was leaving on this trip on this day. Terminal cancer. Saying goodbye to someone forever. My eyes filled with tears remembering sitting at the dinner table sneaking looks at my father, wanting somehow to remember every detail of his hands, his face, his smile.

On the hour ride from Eugene to Corvallis I was absorbed completely in memories of my father's illness and death. I knew that what lay ahead in Seattle would help me understand something about his death. I was profoundly grateful to Sarah for wanting to die embraced by family and friends.

Linda, Leslie, and I left together in a caravan of cars from Corvallis around noon and arrived in Seattle late afternoon. As soon as we stepped off the hospital elevator at Sarah's floor the girls came running down the corridor to greet us. After excited hugs they left to play with two children whose mother was a patient a few doors down from Sarah. Then we saw Patton and, after greetings, went down the hall with him to a sitting area where he told us the latest on Sarah. She was in and out of consciousness. When she was aware, she could listen and speak quite well; it just didn't last very long. Sometimes she was conscious only five to ten seconds, other times minutes. Sarah thought she would die that night.

Leslie and Linda had short visits with Sarah first. When it was my turn, I felt overwhelmed with emotion. It was emotion that didn't have a focus, like an earth tremor that I had absolutely no control over. I hated the emotion intensely. I wanted to be safely in control of myself and I was just the opposite. I walked quickly down the hall away from Patton, Linda and Leslie with my head bowed hoping to find a quick escape before someone saw me. I managed to elude everyone but little Ivana who saw me down the hall and came running to greet me.

"What're you doing?" she asked cheerfully, taking my hand.

"Oh, just looking for a bathroom. Do you know where one is?" I asked.

She smiled broadly and led me to the door of a one-person bathroom hidden away in a corner.

"Thank you, Ivana!" I said sincerely. It was indeed exactly what I was looking for.

I slipped inside and locked the door. Ivana immediately started to jiggle the door knob.

"Sweetie, I need to be alone for awhile, okay?" I said.

"I'll just wait here for you!" Ivana stated happily.

I put the toilet seat down and sat on it, my face in my hands. The tears and sobs came with a force that seemed unstoppable. Ivana continued to knock periodically on the door to see when I was coming out, innocently oblivious to what I was experiencing.

My feelings fluctuated dramatically. First I would berate myself for not being able to control my feelings. *This child is about to lose her mother and I am the one who can't pull herself together.* Then I would be in touch with how much of what had happened over the year I had kept inside and how devastated I felt losing Sarah. My internal voice would soften and give permission for me to feel these emotions that seemed endlessly deep. Anxiety also was present. What is this force that has made it so clear to me what is going to happen?

In an attempt to regain control, I went to the sink to splash cold water on my face. I turned the water on and looked up at myself in the mirror. The emotion that moments before had felt overwhelming suddenly receded as if attached to a zoom lens that was pulled back quickly. I recognized the person in the mirror but I did not identify with this person being me. The feeling was, gosh, it's too bad she feels sad.

I took a few deep breaths and exited to an excited Ivana. She grabbed my hand and I swung her up to carry her. We pressed our faces together and I squished her nose gently with my finger. She giggled.

"I get to go see your mom now," I said smiling.

"Good!" Ivana stated as she wrapped her arms around my neck and pressed her face against mine. Then Ivana heard her sister and friends call for her and she scrambled out of my arms and ran to them.

I walked to Sarah's room and quietly opened the door. When I saw Sarah I almost gasped. She was limp in bed like a rag doll propped up against a pillow. Her eyes were half open in semi-consciousness. Her hair had grown in and looked oddly out of place to me. I was used to Sarah without hair. She had a dark red sore on the end of her tongue like a marble and her mouth and teeth and lips were stained with blood. Her eyes were bruised as if blackened in a fist fight. Occasionally she would startle completely awake, her intense green eyes fully open, focused, and ready.

During one of those moments I said to her the only thing I really wanted to say, "I will always love you."

She replied, "And I you," then closed her eyes, gone again. I sat by Sarah's bed for a few minutes while she slept, then I left the room quietly.

Sarah's sisters arrived that night, first Nancy from California, then Julie from Colorado. Nancy, the doctor, and Julie, the nurse, came well prepared for the situation. I first met Nancy in Sarah's room. Out in the hallway a few minutes later we met again. With a big smile she said, "So you're the one Sarah and Hillary have chosen to be Patton's next wife."

"Yeah, that's me," I smiled back laughing with both relief and embarrassment at hearing something so private expressed so openly.

Jane, Sarah's mother, and Bud, Sarah's step-father, were already there. All of Sarah's family had gathered. A long time friend, Susan, who lived in New York, was supposed to arrive the next morning at eleven. Whether Sarah should try to hold on to see Susan became the focus of discussion between Patton and Sarah.

"I don't know what to do. When will Susan be here?" Sarah would ask Patton.

"Eleven tomorrow morning. Susan would understand, Sarah, if you need to let go. It's okay to let go now. But if you feel like you want to hang on, that's okay too. Either way is okay," Patton would reply. They had many conversations like this through the day.

I could see the pain in Patton's face as he tried to help Sarah.

"She doesn't want to let Susan down. She's flying all the way across the country to see Sarah," Patton said to me.

"Sarah has to know it would be okay to let go. That's a lot more important than flying across the country!" I replied emotionally.

"I know. But Sarah really wants to see Susan and say goodbye."

That evening Linda, Leslie, and I took Hillary and Ivana to dinner at the hospital cafeteria. This was old hat to the girls and they immediately collected the food they wanted for dinner. Later Patton joined us at dinner and we had a lighthearted time telling stories.

After dinner, Leslie, Linda and Patton left for the apartment with the children. The plan was for Patton to help put the kids to bed and then return to the hospital. Leslie and Linda would spend the night with the kids. I would "hold down the fort" at the hospital until Patton returned and then Patton and I would sleep in Sarah's room on two fold out cots.

Patton, Sarah, and I slept sporadically the first night. Sarah's urethra was bleeding as a result of her low platelet count, and it was very painful for her to urinate. She would rouse suddenly from a deep sleep and get out of bed to urinate in the bedside toilet. This made me nervous, and I would watch from my somewhat hidden post in bed as her chin would fall suddenly to her chest when she briefly lost consciousness. Sometimes she would be out of bed every fifteen minutes. Other times the intervals would be as long as an hour. We spoke a few times during the night. Mostly the conversations weren't anything more than, "Are you okay?" and a short reply, "Yes."

Patton and I were exhausted the next morning. After showering and catching everyone up on how the night had gone, we went downstairs to the cafeteria. We went through the cafeteria line, selected food and caffeine for breakfast, and found a booth.

"You know, you were one of the reasons we came out here," Patton said after we had each had a few silent bites and sips.

"Out where?" I replied, not understanding what he meant.

"Sarah was impressed with you when she came out here for a visit. You were one of the people in the department she spoke with. I remember her telling me she liked you. Then later, when we talked about where she should go to school, you came up."

"I had no idea," I replied, feeling surprised. "There's some irony in that, you know," I said shaking my head. "During one of my first visits with Sarah in the hospital back home she told me that she thought the statistics class she took from me had contributed to her illness."

Patton chuckled. "Sounds like Sarah. She really wanted to know why this happened to her."

"Yeah, I know. Sarah's need for an explanation has been one of the hardest things for me to deal with. She is so at peace most of the time, and then her need for an explanation disrupts the peace."

"She likes to be in control," Patton said.

"Yeah, I've noticed," I said returning his grin. "I remember Sarah visiting me in my office after I graded the final exams in my class. She got almost a perfect score, something like ninety-eight percent, and she wanted to know why I had taken off two points! She was mad. It really took me by surprise."

Patton laughed out loud. "I certainly know the feeling! When she wants something, look out."

Our conversation paused as we both ate some of our food.

"I remember very clearly the conversation I had with her when she visited the department," I said breaking the silence. "We sat in the department lounge. She told me she was married to an Episcopal priest. I couldn't believe it!" I said, smiling at Patton. "She didn't seem like a priest's wife to me."

"Ha!" Patton laughed, "I don't think she much fancied herself that way either. I don't really blame her though. It's a pretty tough role to play, and Sarah is nothing if not honest."

"That's for sure!" I replied chuckling, looking up at Patton.

His expression had changed. He was fighting tears, poking his fork at his food.

We sat in silence for a few moments. "I think she's the most honest person I have ever known," I said gently. "It's what makes her so remarkable and sometimes pretty difficult."

Patton nodded, tears welling. "I can't believe it's all about to end. You know, in some ways it's a relief because we finally know. But, I am going to miss her so much," he said quietly as the tears spilled down his cheeks. "Do you know how many bone marrow biopsies she's had?" he continued.

I shook my head, no.

"Twenty-one."

"God," I exhaled.

Patton nodded looking down at his food.

"Sarah's dealt with this illness in a very remarkable way," I said quietly as Patton pushed his food around his plate with his fork. "She's treated it like some kind of incredible journey, giving an open invitation to anyone who wanted to come on board with her. It was very courageous of her."

Patton nodded in agreement. "This last upswing of leukemia brought nurses and doctors to tears. There really is something about Sarah that's special," he said softly.

"There really is, Patton," I replied, as he looked up and met my eyes. "She's had a pretty wonderful husband through this too, you know."

Later that morning Susan arrived. A highly skilled artist with striking long curly red hair, Susan and Sarah had met years earlier when they both were in Europe, Susan pursuing her art, Sarah pursuing her studies. They had been friends ever since and had kept in close contact during Sarah's illness. Sarah had kept one of Susan's glass creations by her bedside throughout her illness. Susan had not seen Sarah, however, since two years before Sarah's diagnosis.

Susan kept her composure when she first visited with Sarah. She wept, however, as soon as the door to Sarah's room was closed behind her. Susan's image of Sarah, she told me through her tears, was of a young, energetic free spirit on an adventure in Europe. It was very hard to reconcile that image with the way her friend now looked.

Little about Sarah's condition changed the rest of the day. One incident I remember with sadness occurred when I was alone in the room with Sarah. Her only means of dealing with the blood in her mouth was to swish water in her mouth and then spit it out. She had a mirror on her bedside table so that she could see whether her teeth and mouth were bloody. In addition to the mirror, there were two cups on the table, one marked "$H_2$0" and the other marked "spit."

Sarah looked into the mirror and groaned when she saw blood caked on her teeth and lips. She reached for the cup marked "H_2O" with her free hand. After swishing the water in her mouth, she became obviously distressed. She looked from the mirror, to the cup in her hand, to me. Before I could react, she began to dribble the spit onto the mirror. I quickly got the other cup and, in as lighthearted way as I could, exchanged the cup for the mirror.

She spit into the cup and turned to me with a sad and concerned expression and stated, "I am crazy."

"No, Sarah, you are *not* crazy," I replied emphatically. "You just made a mistake. That's okay."

"I am crazy," she repeated with genuine distress in her voice.

At that moment her wonderful Italian doctor knocked on the door and walked into the room.

Sarah looked at him and said, "Paulo, I am crazy."

He smiled at her with both compassion for her obvious concern and confusion. "Crazy?" he asked.

"Paulo, I am crazy."

He shook his head not understanding the meaning of the word. Sarah tried to explain what had happened. The explanation was garbled. She could not express the sequence of events. "The mirror. I spit. The blood on the mirror. I missed the cup." She looked at the mirror and at Paulo and tried to explain.

"Loco. I am loco," she blurted.

"No loco, Sarah!" Paulo exclaimed as he understood Sarah's meaning. Their eyes locked in a long gaze, patient and doctor intensely connected in their losing battle.

"Sarah no loco." Paulo repeated seriously, his eyes still meeting Sarah's. Then he turned and left the room.

I ached to make things right, to tell her anyone could have made that mistake or some other lie. She put her head back on the pillow and closed her eyes.

At another time that day, as Sarah came in and out of consciousness, she whispered, "How are Hillary and Ivana?"

"They're doing okay, Sarah," I replied quietly, my maternal energy surging with empathy for Sarah's concern for her children.

Coming fully awake for a moment, eyes wide open, she replied ferociously, "How could they be doing okay?"

I breathed in sharply in response and scrambled for a reply. "You and Patton have done such an incredible job being honest with them, Sarah. I think they understand what's going on. They must be in a great deal of pain, but it's honest, above board pain. That's why I think they are doing okay."

"How could they be doing okay?" she repeated with anger but with rapidly fading energy.

By the time I replied, she was unconscious again.

"They are going to miss you so much Sarah," I said softly. "But you've done everything you could to prepare them. They are going to get through this and be okay."

18

The second night Patton and I spent in Sarah's room was more peaceful than the first although Sarah continued to wake during the night to urinate. Sometimes, instead of using the bedside toilet, she would push her IV pole into the bathroom with her. This seemed miraculous to me. She was barely conscious much of the time but she could manage to walk a few steps to the bathroom and back.

Before dawn, her breathing became labored and it was obvious she was in pain. When the nurse came in on her routine visit, Sarah wanted to know if the pain medication could be lethal if given in big enough doses. The nurse said that Sarah could have as much pain medication as she needed, but that it could not be used intentionally "in that way."

"I am ready," Sarah said, eyebrows furrowed, looking straight into the nurse's eyes.

"The time will come when it is supposed to come. In the mean time you should try to enjoy yourself," the nurse told Sarah. "You don't seem to me to be a down, morose person, Sarah. Don't be gloomy, sitting in your room, waiting to die. Take a walk or ride in a wheelchair to a window or just sit up and enjoy the view from your room, or think of a joke or get someone to tell you a joke," she suggested.

I was angry at the nurse for talking to Sarah like this. It seemed to me that she was trying to tell Sarah how she should feel, an unfair thing to do to someone at any time, much less in these circumstances. How could she possibly know how Sarah was feeling or what she should be doing? Besides, Sarah was being remarkably brave.

The nurse then asked Sarah if she needed more pain medication. Sarah said she did. The nurse asked how much more she needed. It was currently at three and one half. Sarah asked that it be increased to three and three quarters. The nurse explained to Sarah, Patton and me that the pain medication could be increased at any time to make Sarah comfortable and that comfort was of prime importance.

My interpretation of the nurse's "cheer up speech" must have been different from Sarah's, because when the nurse left the room, Sarah called for Patton.

"Tell me a joke," she requested, her voice soft and weak.

Patton tried to tell her a joke but she did not get the punch line. He tried again with no luck. She drifted into a deep sleep.

In the morning Paulo examined Sarah and found small signs of improvement. Patton felt strongly that Sarah should not be told that there was any sign of improvement. He and Sarah had existed on a roller coaster for too long. He absolutely did not want Sarah to climb aboard again.

By early afternoon Sarah's condition was obviously worsening. The medical staff decided it was essential that Sarah have a catheter. They had resisted to this point because Sarah did not want one and because there was some danger the insertion would increase her bleeding. I was tense until I knew that it had been inserted successfully. Then a heaviness settled in me as I realized that there was no longer any reason for Sarah to move from the bed in which she would die.

Later that afternoon Nancy, Julie, Patton, and I were in Sarah's room. The other three were talking with each other. I looked over at Sarah who was fully awake. Our eyes met in true recognition of each other and my hand went to my heart in our now familiar gesture of caring.

"You are a good friend," she said softly.

I told her I loved her and she replied that she loved me too, then patted the side of the bed, inviting me to sit with her. The others had observed our interaction and were silent as we arranged the tubes coming from Sarah so that I could sit. Once I was seated, she made a motion for my hand and I reached for hers. At first I felt conflicted touching her. Not touching Sarah to protect her from infection was a rule I had gotten used to. Touching her meant that the rules didn't matter any more. One more piece of evidence that she would die soon. Then our eyes met again and I was glad to be connected through touch.

"Hillary and Ivana love you," she stated quietly.

I was silent for a moment as we stared at each other. "I love them too," I replied.

Sarah nodded. We both knew the truth was being stated because there was no time left.

"Patton loves you too and he should tell you," she said in a somewhat annoyed tone as if she couldn't understand what was taking him so long.

We continued our intense eye contact. This time I was the one to nod in reply.

"It's going to be soon," she said.

"Yes," I agreed.

"It seems a little like birth," I said, "focused inward."

She frowned and nodded.

"Patton now," Sarah said.

"You want me to go and Patton to sit here?" I asked.

"Yes," Sarah replied, closing her eyes.

I stood up and Patton positioned himself on the other side of the bed.

Their conversation did not last more than a sentence or two as Sarah was becoming very tired. Nancy suggested that we should all leave so that Sarah could rest.

"Not so close," Sarah said, seemingly in response to Nancy's suggestion.

"You want us here but not so close to you?" I asked.

"Yes," she replied softly as she drifted away.

We stayed and chatted with each other. My external self joined the conversation. My internal self, however, was engaged in trying to find a place not only for Sarah's impending death but also for the crescendo of feelings that had been building for many months concerning my role in this drama.

19

Early in the evening Sarah decided she wanted a party with her family and friends. Julie and I went to the hospital cafeteria where the others had gone for a snack.

"Meet in Sarah's room, she wants a party," we announced smiling.

They looked at each other with surprised expressions and then said, "Okay, we're on our way!"

We gathered in Sarah's room and kidded Sarah about the keg of beer that would arrive soon for her party. Sarah's family began to tell stories. The focus was on an island they own in northern Minnesota that had been the location of many family summers and honeymoons. Sarah seemed to enjoy the positive energy and her family seemed more relaxed than I had seen them. "This is a wake, a time to remember shared experiences," I thought as I listened to the stories. I was glad for this time for everyone.

The rest of the evening, Sarah was conscious for only very brief periods. Occasionally, in an effort that seemed incredible to me, she would sit straight up and attempt to stabilize herself by putting her hands on the bed behind her, locking her arms. She would quickly lose consciousness and her head would fall forward and she would lean far to one side or the other. At least once that evening I watched as Patton held Sarah after she had sat up. He rubbed her back and massaged her scalp. Another time Julie did the same.

Later that night, shortly after Patton and I had put on the hospital scrubs we had been using as night wear, Sarah sat straight up in bed again. We both responded by getting out of bed quickly and holding her, one of us on each side of the bed. We rubbed her back, stroked her hair and massaged her scalp. She communicated that she was ready to lay down by pushing backward and we gently lowered her.

Patton and I got back into our beds. I lay in bed, wide awake, desperately anxious. What if she sits up and falls over, out of the bed? Sarah stirred and Patton and I both responded.

"I can't possibly sleep. I am so afraid that Sarah will need something and no one will be there. We'll be asleep and she won't be able to call a nurse. What if she sits up and falls out of bed?" I said softly, my throat tight with fighting tears.

"The rails are up. I don't think that would happen," Patton replied, slightly taken aback by my emotional response.

"I do!" I said, feeling ferociously protective of Sarah.

Then I started to cry softly and Patton put his arm around me. The experience of finding my father felt very near. "What if Sarah fell?" The thought was unbearable. I needed to get out of the room, feel these long ago feelings, and try to find some perspective.

Patton said he really needed some sleep. I slipped out of the room and walked down a hallway that was temporarily closed. At the end of the hall was a window. I sat on the window sill and, staring out at the Seattle night, relived the horror of finding my father. Then I walked to the family waiting room and lay on the couch, aware that my perspective was quickly shifting from past to present. After awhile I walked back to Sarah's room and quietly slipped inside.

I lay down on my fold out bed, closed my eyes and tried to find a comfortable position. I was wide awake but the feeling of panic had subsided. Then I heard Sarah rustle in bed and I looked over as she sat straight up. I hurried out of bed and caught her as she was tilting over to the other side of the bed. I pulled her back to a centered position and put my arm around her chest so that her chin rested in the crook of my elbow. I hesitantly laid my other hand on her back. I felt very uneasy and awkward standing there, holding Sarah. I was intensely aware of "the rules" of what I was doing. *Was this appropriate? What if a nurse walks in? Should I be doing this?* I asked myself in staccato succession. I couldn't think why this could be wrong, but I was afraid that, somehow, I was breaking a rule I didn't even know existed.

Then, in a moment's shift of awareness, I began to feel the warmth of Sarah's body on my own body, the softness of her skin beneath the thin hospital gown, the sensation in my muscles as I supported her, and I stopped asking questions. I began massaging her back, kneading her muscles, rubbing her scalp. I told her quietly that I knew everything would be okay, that she was doing a great job, that we loved her, that we would be fine even though we would miss her.

As I talked and massaged Sarah, I began to feel as if the space around me was closing and enveloping me in a circular tunnel that I could "see," not through my eyes but rather in my head like something remembered. Then I began to travel through the tunnel. At first the tunnel was narrow and constricting but it expanded rapidly. I seemed to grow with the tunnel, filling it. As I expanded with the tunnel, I moved with increasing speed until I was traveling with tremendous, uninhibited energy. There seemed no bounds to the size of the tunnel, my ability to expand within it, or the speed with which I could travel.

"Sarah, I don't know why our lives crossed like this," I said softly, the energy intensifying every moment. "I wish I understood better. Knowing you has changed me. Thank you. I will always love you and think about you."

Then the feeling of love began to grow. It outgrew the boundaries of love for Sarah. It grew bigger and bigger, huge and all-encompassing. It became love of all the details of life, even the mundane and painful parts. It was love of being alive, of the wonder of existence, and even of the mystery of dying. Everything felt connected to everything else. Death felt connected to life, pain felt connected to joy, evil felt connected to good and it seemed all right that Sarah was dying because she was still connected to me and to everything else.

"Just know you are loved, Sarah," I said quietly.

Then I was no longer in the tunnel.

I noticed that my legs were shaking with the tension of leaning over the bed. I thought about waking Patton but I knew he needed to sleep, and I kept thinking Sarah would want to lie back down any minute. When I asked her if she was ready to lie down, however, she resisted. I kept stroking and talking. My body burned. Then, as suddenly as she had gotten up, she pushed backward, and I lay her head gently on the pillow.

I stood by Sarah's bed watching her breathe, open mouthed, deeply asleep. It was almost a year to the day after the dream with my father. Love is all that matters. Heaven and earth are mirror images. What is reflected is love. Love connects heaven and earth. Love connects life and death. I seemed to breathe in the memory of the dream.

"Sarah, you are going to a good place. I am certain of it. Everything really is going to be okay," I said quietly to my friend.

I returned to my bed physically exhausted and, as had occurred so many times in the last year, emotionally stunned by an experience that seemed to push back the boundaries of the life I had known. Before I could get to sleep, Sarah's breathing changed dramatically. Patton and I were both by her bed asking each other if she was in pain. It seemed obvious to both of us that she was. She was restless and her breathing was labored and uneven.

We called the nurse who was new to Sarah. The nurse suggested that we give Sarah boosts of pain medication. Sarah was hooked via an IV to a machine that not only dispensed a steady flow of pain medication but also had a button that, when pushed, would dispense a boost of pain medication. The machine was programmed to allow these boosts every eight minutes. We tried one boost which did not seem to make a difference so we inquired about increasing the steady flow of pain medication. The nurse's immediate reaction was that she could not do this because it was not on the chart. I cursed the fact that this, of all nights, Sarah would get such a "stick to the rules" idiot. I was furious but tried to keep my temper. I told her that the previous night the nurse had told us the pain medication could be increased whenever we wanted and by however much Sarah needed. The nurse said the only way she could increase meds was if it was on Sarah's chart and she was quite sure it wasn't on the chart. Then she said she would go get the chart just to make sure.

She returned with the chart as proof that she could not increase the pain medication. I repeated what the other nurse had said. I was beginning to feel out of control. I wanted to tell her that if she wouldn't increase the meds, then leave the room and we would figure out how to do it ourselves. The nurse said the only thing she could think of to do was to ask the on call doctor. She left again as Patton and I kept track of each eight minute interval, punching the button within seconds after each interval. When the nurse returned she said that, indeed, the pain medication could be increased at any time and for any amount.

After the medication was increased, Sarah seemed to rest without pain. Her eyes were open even as she appeared to be deeply asleep. The nurse explained that she had lost control of her eyelid muscles. She also said that when there is some hope of resuscitating a patient, efforts are made to protect the eyes but that in Sarah's situation this was not necessary.

Sarah's breathing was becoming increasingly shallow and rapid. The sound of her breathing was different than any breathing I had ever heard, raspy and hollow. She would maintain the same breathing pattern for a few minutes and then it would change. Around 6:30 Sarah's sister, Nancy, stopped by the room. She had to leave at 7:15 to catch a plane home. After staying two or three minutes, Nancy left to get her sister and Susan who were staying in a room three floors down.

Nancy, Julie, and Susan were soon in the room. Sarah's breathing became increasingly rapid. Her heart was racing. Patton was near Sarah's face, talking quietly to her. Nancy and Julie were standing on either side of Sarah's bed. Susan and I sat together on my bed watching

Sarah silently. All of a sudden Sarah's breathing became very shallow and slow. Someone said "she will die soon." Her breaths became barely audible. Then she was still. It was five minutes after seven, Friday, June sixteenth.

Patton and Susan cried in each other's arms briefly and then turned to Sarah. Patton said that he had felt Sarah's spirit leave her body when her breathing stopped. One second she was present and the next second she was not.

Nancy, Julie and I focused quietly on Sarah. Her body was cool to the touch and had a distinctly grayish tint. Her mouth was half-way open, still in the circle of her last breath. Blood from mouth sores stained her teeth and lips. Her eyes were open and staring. Her arms rested at her sides and her head was tilted on the pillow toward the door as if expecting someone to arrive. None of this seemed difficult to absorb. But the stillness of her body I could not comprehend. I kept expecting movement. I didn't watch for big movements of head or arms, but I couldn't get used to looking at her chest and not seeing slight heart flutters or subtle rhythms of breathing. I felt startled when she continued to be so still. A small part of me was worried that she was uncomfortable staying still for so long.

As I watched Sarah's body, trying to absorb the reality of the physical differences between life and death, I was deeply in touch with a duality of awareness. I was both stunned by the reality that I would never have contact with Sarah's physical being again and, at the same time, anchored in the serene stillness of knowing that her death simply was and that we would always truly be connected to each other.

Nancy announced that she had to leave in order to catch a plane home. After a last goodbye to Sarah, she left. Patton, Susan, Julie, and I stayed in the room and talked. We all kept looking over to Sarah as if it would be rude to exclude her from our conversation.

Then, one by one, we left the room for various reasons. I left for a much needed drink of water. When I returned, Patton was preparing to call Hillary and Ivana's baby-sitter to let her know that he would be coming over. He asked me to call in case one of the children answered. He did not want to chance having to tell the girls over the phone that their mother had died. The baby-sitter answered, and I passed the phone to Patton. He arranged to be there soon.

After he left, Susan and Julie returned to the room. Julie's extroverted energy was contagious and the three of us chatted easily. I began to clean up, taking the sheets off of Patton's bed and folding up the bed, peeling pictures off the wall, collecting paper cups and throwing them away.

At one point the conversation turned to the pragmatics of getting Patton and the girls back to Corvallis. I offered that, if the timing was right, I could drive back up with a rental truck. Mid-sentence I was blindsided by a memory and suddenly began to sob. Poor Julie was confused and concerned. "What's wrong, are you okay?" she kept saying. I turned away, slightly embarrassed and more than slightly startled by the power and suddenness of these emotions. I tried to explain that this had been the plan just a few weeks ago when all looked well and Sarah had been told she and her family could return home. I was going to rent a truck in Corvallis and drive up to Seattle. Patton would drive the family car and I would drive the truck back down to Corvallis since Sarah could not drive. I attempted to tell them all of this but it came out in confusing bits as I tried to regain control. Then the emotion passed, I took a deep breath, turned around and, tear stained, told them what I had been struggling to say.

A few minutes later two nurses came in and asked gently if it was time to remove the body. We said yes. They misunderstood my slight hesitation to move as desire to watch them go through the process of removing the body, which they advised against. I did not want to watch.

After leaving a note to Patton on the door, Susan and I went to the cafeteria. We sat quietly, sharing the experience mostly in silence yet feeling connected to each other's feelings and thoughts. After awhile Susan went to her room to pack and I checked to see if Patton had returned to Sarah's room. He had returned just a few minutes before me.

We found a few boxes and a cart and packed up Sarah's possessions. In the process of packing Patton occasionally would come across something that would make him stop and stare and remember. I wanted to be there as a support but not to interfere with his process of saying goodbye to this final place he had lived with his wife.

We loaded the car, drove to the apartment, and unloaded the boxes. Then the phone started to ring. Patton would talk a long while to someone, hang up the phone, come out of the room to say a few words to me, and then the phone would ring again. This pattern lasted all afternoon. By dinner time Patton decided he would just have to ignore the phone and leave if we were ever going to have dinner.

We decided to take a walk along the waterfront before eating. As we strolled, Patton talked about parts of his past that I had not heard. He spoke of scattered segments of his life as if he was a quilter surveying squares of fabric before deciding how to put them together. There was a stint in the Navy, churches in the south and New England, the beginnings of his relationship with Sarah, a trip to Europe, training in a V.A. hospital, children being born, work as a psychotherapist, and writing his books. We sat on a bench overlooking the water, silently watching the water lap the shore.

"This reminds me a lot of Vancouver," I said comforted by the feeling of familiarity with the place I had lived as a teen and where my mother and two of my three siblings still lived.

"Vancouver is wonderful," Patton replied. "I would love to visit it again some time."

"We'll have to take a trip up there together. My mother really enjoys company. She'd especially like you I am sure. She could tell all her friends an Episcopal priest was staying at her house," I said, poking Patton in the shoulder playfully.

"Yes, I am a popular guy," he replied smiling.

We decided to dine at a Chinese restaurant that Patton particularly liked. On the drive to the restaurant I could feel a slow swell of anxiety building in my gut. When are we going to talk about Sarah's plan for us to be in a relationship? I needed to at least say something aloud, to prick a hole in this balloon that had been expanding for months.

We parked, walked to the restaurant and put our names on the waiting list. We were told there would be a fifteen minute wait.

"Well, what should we do while we wait?" Patton asked.

My chest and throat tightened as I mustered the courage to broach the topic I so needed to talk about.

"Well, maybe we should talk about Sarah's little plan that the two of us should get into a relationship," I said. Once the words were spoken, I was amazed at how suddenly relaxed I felt. I laughed and said, "No biggy, but it's probably something we should talk about some time."

"I'm glad you brought it up. If you hadn't, I would have. Yes, indeed, it is something we need to talk about. Do you want to go first and tell me how you are feeling about this?"

"No, I'd rather you tell me how you are feeling," I replied.

"Okay. Well, as you already know, I think Sarah made a very good choice. She always was good at sizing a person up and I think she was right this time too. The truth is, though, it's really hard for me to imagine being in a relationship. I need some time. I have a lot of decisions to make about just about everything in my life. Little things like where to live, how to make a living, where the kids should go to school, how to single parent; everything is up in the air.

"I'd also be afraid if we were in a relationship that I couldn't grieve this loss. How would you feel if we were in a relationship and I was sad about Sarah? It seems like that would cause problems. So, how are you feeling about all of this?"

"You have expressed exactly what I am feeling too. You and the girls are already very important to me, but the timing for a relationship certainly is not right. I know you have to make a lot of really big decisions. I think we are seeing things basically the same way. There is something you need to know though, Patton. I could never imagine in a million years not understanding your loss. I loved her too, you know. I miss her too. I never ever want you to feel like you can't express your grief about Sarah around me, no matter what kind of relationship we have."

"Well that's good to hear," Patton said smiling at me. "And I do know you loved Sarah too."

—20—

I left Seattle three days after Sarah died. Patton and the girls stayed an additional week, packing their belongings with the help of Sarah's sister and parents.

I called my mother the night I returned home. "This has been a life changing experience for me, Mom. I was there when she died. I felt certain she was going to a good, loving place. I feel a great deal of loss but, in another way it's hard to describe, it's like life and death just simply are. Things are as they are supposed to be and there is peace in that."

My mother was oddly silent, as if her serious contemplation of what I had said needed time. "Death can be very life giving," she said, breaking the silence. "I know that from the experiences I have had with friends dying. I feel sad for Patton and the girls though. This is a tremendous loss for them. How are they?"

"They seem remarkably fine now. I don't know, and Patton is certainly not sure, whether this will last. We'll just have to wait and see what the process is."

"Well, I do think this will be very hard on the girls," she said gently.

Patton's plan after returning to Oregon was to spend some time organizing their home.

Then he and the girls would travel for a month in his camper.

After a few days at home, Patton decided he needed to have a large garage sale to lighten what he felt was a burden of material possessions. I was there to help the morning of the sale. That was the first time the girls called me mom. Hillary said it first in a hesitant, teasing kind of way, obviously looking for my reaction. I simply answered the question she had asked me. After that, every other word it seemed out of both girls was "mom." They were trying on this new phenomenon from every angle available.

That evening, Patton and the girls took me out to dinner to thank me for helping with the garage sale. I carried Ivana up the stairs at the restaurant because she wanted to be close.

"Do you know why Hillary and me call you mom?" she asked.

"No, why?"

"Because we want to call somebody mom," she stated.

"Yes, I do understand that, Ivana," I replied, hugging her tight.

"What the hell are they calling you mom for?" Zach demanded, his eyes flashing anger.

"You're *our* mom!" Corey added with equal rage.

I hesitated for a moment, caught in a mother's conflict between reprimanding Zach for his language and knowing that his language expressed heartfelt emotion.

"Guys, listen to me," I began. "Ivana told me that she and Hillary call me mom because they want to call someone mom. Can you try to understand a little bit what it would be like to not have anybody to call mom?" I asked.

"But you are *not* their mom," Corey stated concretely, his anger only slightly abated.

"We don't care what you say. We don't want them calling you mom," Zach said, taking over as spokesman for the pair.

"It would feel pretty weird to have someone call your own mom 'mom'," I replied, reaching out to Zach. He put his hand up for a moment then lowered it, and they both melted into my arms.

I was visiting Patton and the girls a few days later when I realized I had lost track of time and needed to be somewhere else quickly. I jogged upstairs to where the girls were playing, said a quick goodbye to each of them, and then jogged back down the stairs. Patton was already outside. In the middle of a quick goodbye to Patton, we both stopped and listened. We could hear Ivana sobbing hysterically through the open window upstairs. Patton and I looked at each other.

"Did you say goodbye to Ivana?" he asked.

"I did. It was pretty fast though," I said, turning to go back inside to see what had happened. I went up the stairs two at a time, hearing Ivana's increasingly distressed cry. When I reached her she screamed in-between sobs, "You didn't say goodbye!"

I scooped her up. "You hate it when someone leaves without telling you goodbye," I stated.

"Yes," she said inhaling sharply between sobs.

"You know, I did come upstairs to say goodbye but maybe you didn't hear me. I said it pretty fast because I was in a hurry," I continued.

I sat on the floor and held her until her sobs had stopped.

"From now on I will try hard to say a really good goodbye to you when I leave. Is that a deal?"

"Yes," she said, getting off my lap, smiling broadly.

"Well, come here then for a big goodbye because I have to go." She came over and we gave each other noisy hugs.

"I'll see you soon, okay?" I said, letting go of Ivana.

"Okay!" she replied happily.

It became obvious, upon returning from Seattle, that not only had the external circumstances of my life changed, so had the internal circumstances. The ceiling of my previous world had been lifted to reveal a vastness that I had never known. Relative to the vastness, all that had seemed familiar now seemed different. What had been true now seemed relatively true. Even my grief, that at times felt overwhelmingly real, at other times seemed only to be the human foible of living within the constraints I had created.

This tremendous change of awareness made demands I could not ignore. I found that the balance between having energy to function and being totally depleted could tip in an instant over an unpleasant interaction between my children, unloading one more glass from the dishwasher after I was ready to stop, or doing an extra errand. Oddly, when the balance was in my favor, I felt fairly normal, but as soon as the scales tipped, I would feel unable to cope with even the normal occurrences of everyday life. I quickly became acutely aware of maintaining the balance in my favor by paying close attention to my energy level, something I had been used to virtually ignoring in my usual busy life.

I also found that a new internal part of me now put all of life's activities into two distinct categories: activities I had energy for and which gave me energy, and activities I had no energy for and which drained me completely. Being at home with my children, relating to others with whom I had a sincere relationship, and being in nature fell into the first category. Engaging in anything that felt inauthentic fell into the second category.

By far the most distressing aspect of this change was that this new part of me put my career into the second category. I had labored for years as a graduate student and assistant professor, pursuing work that I felt passionate about. I had never wavered in my belief that I was doing what I was supposed to be doing: teaching and conducting research on human development. Now, I felt a very strong internal distancing from anything having to do with my work. It was terrifying. I was going up for tenure in a year and I had counted on writing research papers, so central to academic success, over the summer. Now, every time I tried to work, I was stopped completely by lack of motivation and energy. My rational mind tried to argue with whatever internal force was creating these strong feelings. I soon learned, however, what a hopeless and depleting fight this was. Thoughts of how long I had worked for tenure, or how much my career meant to me were simply absorbed without impact.

Another change was that stillness became an essential need in my life, as compelling as thirst. I would find ways to be alone; then I would sit, staring ahead, absorbing sights, sounds and smells in a vast new emptiness inside of me that did not have to think, but could just be. I had to find this stillness frequently, if only for a short while, or I simply could not function.

In the days and then weeks after Sarah's death, I awoke every morning feeling like my life was no longer familiar to me. Little did I know that events just ahead would deepen my understanding of all that I had learned through Sarah's illness and death.

21

The phone call from my mother was in early July, only a few weeks after Sarah died. She called in the middle of the week, which was rare unless there was something special she wanted to tell me or some occurrence in my life she wanted to know about sooner than her regular Sunday call.

"Don't worry, honey," my mother slurred as soon as I picked up the phone. "I'll be better soon. See Jon just thought I should," she said referring to my brother. "They said it was potassium or calcium, can't remember. One week. Feeling very tired. Nothing to worry."

"Whoa, Mom, you're not making any sense!" I said reflexively, completely surprised by this sudden change in my mother.

"Start again from the beginning. I think you are assuming I know things I don't know. Where did you go?"

She laughed awkwardly. "Emergency room. Jon took me."

"Jon took you to the emergency room? Why, Mom?" I asked urgently.

"Oh, nothing to worry about. It will go away in a week. Nothing to worry about," she stated slowly and haltingly, as if drunk but trying to hide her condition.

"Mom, I *am* worried. What's wrong?" I said emphatically, verbally taking her by the shoulders and demanding a straight explanation.

"Honey, everything is fine. I'll be better. End of week. Sorry this is coming out like this. I am very tired."

"I'm sure everything is fine, Mom. Is Jon there?"

"No, not now, later. I need a nap. I need to go now," she said, sounding as if she was already half asleep.

When we hung up I was totally perplexed but, oddly, not overly worried. What in the world was that about? I asked myself. I look back at that conversation and wonder at my reaction. Despite the fact that my intelligent and articulate mother was totally disoriented and nonsensical, I dismissed it as being nothing to worry about. Any intuitive wisdom I had was completely shut down. I simply could not believe that something could be seriously wrong with my mother so soon after all I had experienced with Sarah.

Jon called later that day. "I need to talk to you about Mom," he said.

"Yeah, what's going on? I got the weirdest phone call from her. You took her to the emergency room? Why?"

"She has been acting extremely tired, falling asleep all the time during the day and she is very confused and disoriented. They did some blood work at the hospital and found out that she has extremely low potassium. That can cause these symptoms. They have her on potassium and it's supposed to help by the end of the week. It's been hard around here. She has really been acting different. I keep thinking about this one thing that happened. She fell and hit her head against her dresser. I don't know if she fainted or tripped but it left quite a knot. You know Mom though, she kept saying it was nothing."

"It sounds to me like we should probably be more worried about why she fell than the knot itself, don't you think?"

"Yes, exactly."

"Why would her potassium be so low?" I asked.

"The doctors in the emergency room were furious at the combination of medicines she was taking. That idiot doctor she has been going to for twenty years. We just need to tell her she cannot go there anymore, period!"

"Ha, good luck!" I said referring to our mother's irrational attachment to this man she admitted was a lousy doctor.

"Well Lord knows I have tried everything," Jon said dejectedly. "I finally concluded it really is her life and her decision."

"Yeah, that's a side of Mom I sure don't understand. Listen, I'll call in a couple of days to see how things are going."

"Okay, bye."

I heard from my sister, Mary, next. "The problem is, she doesn't remember to take her potassium. She would never take it if Jon or I didn't give it to her and watch her take it. She has lost her ability to reason. All she can do is make choices between two things. I took her to the grocery store and she went through with me saying, do you want apple or orange juice, turkey or chicken? She liked it; it was a game, sort of. We had a good time together. It's weird, but she is wonderful to be around. She is loving and sweet and we laugh even though I don't think we always know what we're laughing about.

"You know, it wasn't more than three weeks ago that she took the bus all the way to my place for Margie's dance recital. I remember thinking at the time that she was showing a few subtle signs of aging. She's so completely different now, it's unbelievable."

"Wow Mary, could all of this really be about low potassium?"

"I don't know. It seems like maybe she had a stroke. Although extremely low potassium can have these types of effects."

"I guess we'll know more soon, when the potassium has done its thing."

"Could you come up sometime? Mom really should not be alone and it's a lot for Jon and me to manage. I am really afraid she could leave a burner going on the stove."

"Yeah, I could. Let me make arrangements and I'll call you back tomorrow."

Mom showed only slight improvement over the following days. I talked to her on the phone every day. The conversations were strange and painful, punctuated by long pauses, non-sequesters, incomplete sentences, and, occasionally, a perfectly normal sentence.

Mary took her to another doctor who thought the cause of her disorientation could be a series of mini strokes or a major stroke. The doctor arranged for Mom to be thoroughly diagnosed at a well-known clinic the following week. We were anxious for a diagnosis, in part, because a big family reunion was about to occur in Tennessee and we wanted to know whether Mom would be able to attend. All of our extended family on my mother's side was gathering to celebrate the one hundredth anniversary of a family home built by my great grandfather and his family on the side of Lookout Mountain. We had all looked forward to it, but none of us as much as my mother.

"No matter what we find out about what's wrong with Mom, it is absolutely out of the question that she travel alone," Mary told me on the phone. "She can't negotiate around the grocery store, much less through an airport. One of us will have to travel with her. I don't think anyone should say anything about the reunion to her though. I really don't think she remembers that it's happening. I don't know what to do."

"What if this is a stroke? And what if it happens again when she's traveling?" my brother asked when we talked. We all agreed to wait until the following Thursday, when Mom was scheduled to enter the clinic, before making a final decision about the reunion.

The Sunday before Mom was to enter the clinic, Mary drove in to pick up Mom so that Mom could stay with her for a few days. Jon took Mom to church in the morning and returned convinced that he and Mary needed to take her to the hospital emergency room immediately. She was extremely disoriented and virtually unresponsive.

Mary called that night. "They did a C.A.T. scan and found a brain tumor," she stated immediately, with a quiet tension in her voice.

"Oh no," I said, breathless. My first thought was that it was Mary who had called me all those years ago to tell me that Dad had been diagnosed with cancer. Then an inner quiet that comes with the knowledge that something has happened that will forever be important settled in me. Within that quiet I looked for an explanation for how this could be happening when I was still grieving Sarah's death. Disbelief that the universe could be so unfair melted into the reality that this actually was happening. The two coexisted, partly merged, as I asked for more details. "What else did they say, Mary?"

"They're not saying whether it is malignant. It's big though. It's in both sides of her brain and it is not operable. The doctor said the long term prognosis is not good and that she will eventually die from the tumor."

I felt like falling to the floor. The person who had always been there, the person who had always cared about all of the details of my life, who understood and loved my children, how could she go away? The truth of my separateness, that I had glimpsed in the grocery store, seemed to come out of hiding like a petrifying event I had been able to suppress until now.

"It's malignant. It's got to be!" I stated in a voice louder and stronger than I had intended.

"Will they do a biopsy?" I asked.

"They haven't said."

"Mary, if a doctor tells you that she will die of this, it is serious. They don't go out on that kind of limb without a reason."

"Yeah, I agree."

"Well, how are they going to treat it?"

"They haven't said yet."

"I'm coming up soon."

"Listen, since you can't spend all summer up here, why don't you wait until she's out of the hospital. Things are reasonably under control here now, but we will really need you when she gets out."

"Okay, let's talk tomorrow."

The next two days my two sisters, my brother, and I spent hours on the phone with each other and with my mother's sister and three brothers who were scattered across the U.S. What does it mean to have an inoperable brain tumor? She can't go to the reunion, that's a certainty. So now we learn how to deal with our mother functioning at a lower level. Okay, we do that. I refused to believe that my mother would no longer be in my life.

Mary called on Wednesday to tell me that further tests had revealed that Mom had a glioblastoma, one of the most aggressive, invasive types of brain tumors. The team of cancer doctors had assessed treatment options and had strongly recommended that no treatment be given. The tumor had already spread too far for any treatment to be effective

I broke down on the phone with Mary. Then I called my twin sister, Peggy, in North Carolina, just as I had called to tell her of our father's death.

"Oh God, I've got to get out there right away. I'll get a flight and call you back."

"Okay."

Patton, Hillary, Ivana and my children were in another part of the house. I poked my head out the bedroom door where I had been talking on the phone and motioned for Patton to come in. He looked at my face and said, "Oh no, it's bad news."

I couldn't talk. I just nodded my head. *This is not fair. I can't handle this right now. It can't be happening*. I kept saying to myself. My sense of justice was badly bruised. I was still not fully functioning after Sarah's death. I had tried so hard to be open through that experience. And this was my reward!

"It's too much!" I sobbed into Patton's shoulder then walked over to a laundry basket on the floor and kicked it half-way across the room. I walked into the adjoining bathroom and broke down completely. Patton waited for me to emerge.

"It's one of the most aggressive kinds of tumors. Oh God, Patton, this can't be happening."

Then the phone rang. It was Peggy. She had made arrangements to fly into Eugene that night. We would pick her up from the airport and make the eight hour drive to Vancouver together.

"Mommy, what's wrong?" my children asked when they saw my red, swollen eyes.

"Grandmom is very, very sick. We are going to pick up Aunt Peggy at the airport tonight and drive up to Vancouver."

"Is she going to die?"

"Yes, she is."

"No!" my eldest son wailed as his legs sagged and he knelt to the floor. "No, she can't! Not Grandmom."

I pulled him in and tried to hold his pain.

"Will she die when we are there?" my younger son wanted to know.

"I don't know but I think she probably will," I replied.

He just stared at me and I drew him close too.

I called my ex-husband at work to tell him what was happening. He asked if I needed him to take the boys for a few hours so that I could get ready for the trip. I said yes, it would be a great help. He had loved my mother dearly, adopting her as the perfect mother and grandmother figure. She had lived up to his expectations. Her many long visits with our family had always been eagerly awaited by all. It had been good for my relationship with my mother for me to see her through my husband's and children's adoring eyes.

After the boys left with their father, I quickly made plans to be away for an unknown period. I called a teenage neighbor to look after the animals, and a friend at work to spread word that I would be away for awhile. What to pack? Oh God! What to pack to say goodbye to my mother? You don't say goodbye to your mother. It seemed absurd. I wanted to shout: "This doesn't happen! Mommies are always there, you count on mommies, they don't leave." I felt embarrassed by these feelings, as if caught in a grocery store with a tantruming child. But the child was too furious to be subdued. "Don't leave!" she screamed. "What am I supposed to do without you?"

Over the next weeks I would shake my head in disbelief many times as I tried to find something to wear each morning. I had packed one pair of shorts and one pair of jeans that I would wear day after day, and an absurd number of panty hoses to go with two skirts.

After I finished arranging for the trip, I lay down on the couch and Patton sat next to me.

"Tell me a what a perfect day would be for you," I said to Patton.

I closed my eyes as he described rising late, a rich breakfast, a long walk on the beach followed by leisurely shopping and a walk in the woods, then dinner and live entertainment.

"You know what I want to do sometime?" I asked him. "I want to snorkel somewhere in crystal clear warm water and just float and swim and look at all the wonderful sea life."

"Let's do that," he replied.

After our brief rest, I said goodbye to Patton and the girls. Patton's plan was to finish packing for their trip that afternoon and to leave early the next morning.

Peggy was already off the plane and at the baggage claim when we arrived at the airport. "There she is!" Zach shouted when he saw his aunt.

We embraced extra hard and, without saying very much, walked briskly to my car and settled in to drive as far as we could that night. We talked easily as always on the drive. I was very glad to be in the company of someone who was as stunned and disoriented as I was. No explanations were necessary, only comforting comparisons of feelings.

Something had been wrong with my car for a long time. It jerked badly at certain speeds. Three garages had not been able to fix it. When it started jerking on the way to Vancouver, Peggy looked at me and laughed.

"Sorry," I said, "nobody can figure out what's wrong."

She put her hand to her mouth as if holding a radio transmitter. "Crrrr crrrrrr," she made the sound of radio static. "We're coming in for a bumpy landing. Please hold on to your children and fasten your seat belts."

I started laughing then she laughed then we laughed harder and harder until I pleaded, "Stop! I'm going to pee my pants!"

This made her laugh even harder. How many times in our lives had we done this? Countless. As I laughed, I recalled the last time this had happened, a couple of years before. She had been driving that time. I had simply asked if she had a memory of Mom or Dad saying the words "I love you" to her. Her immediate reaction had been "Of course I do." Then I asked her to tell me what the circumstance had been. She had pondered and pondered then looked at me and we had both burst into hysterical laughter.

"No," she had squeaked out amidst gut heaving laughter. Between groans, we both agreed that we had felt very loved but neither of us could conjure one memory of those words from our parents. We had laughed so hard she had driven onto the gravel shoulder of the road where she managed to stop as we continued laughing so long that tears streamed down our faces.

We stopped at a motel between Portland and Seattle at two in the morning. The boys sleep-walked to our room. I lay awake, trying to convince myself that we were doing what it seemed we were doing: going home to say goodbye to Mom. I must have slept because I remember waking up. It was five thirty. I looked at Peggy whose eyes were open.

"Could you sleep any more?" I whispered to her.

"No, I'm wanting to get going," she replied.

"Me too."

As we continued on the trip, I thought about arriving at the hospital. What will Mom look like? How will I stay in control when I see her? Will the hospital be like the one in Seattle where Sarah had been? At first everything will seem strange and foreign, I told myself. Then, soon, it will all begin to seem familiar. I knew this too well. Sarah had been dead just over a month.

—22—

Mom was in a room with three other women, all of whom were in hospital for back surgery. I looked into the room. Mary and her two teen-age daughters, Lynde and Margie, were by Mom's bed. I saw Mom. Her hair was straight and falling into her eyes. I had never seen her hair without a once-a-week-to-the-hairdresser perm. She looked a bit like a mental patient or a derelict, someone who was not able or did not care to groom herself properly.

Suddenly I was acutely aware of being in great danger of losing all control. I felt exposed and panicked as I turned quickly to leave. Mary saw me and gave me a hug. Head lowered, I slid down the hall and slipped into a one-person bathroom. The similarity with arriving at the hospital to say goodbye to Sarah made me woozy; I wanted to spit on the floor to get the taste of knowing what was coming out of my mouth. My skin was hot and my joints ached like I had a fever.

I sobbed as quietly as I could, wanting to get this part over with. Heaves of sorrow. I valued my relationship with my mother so much. I enjoyed it and gained so much from it. It was unique in my life. As I cried, loss spilled out. It splashed over until it was once again contained. I washed my face with cold water and took a few deep breaths. I looked in the mirror like I did in the bathroom in the Seattle hospital. All I saw was me.

As I walked down the hallway to my mother, I was aware of every sensation in my body: the heaviness in my feet, the dryness in my mouth, the sting in my eyes, the constriction in my heart.

"You can do it," I said to myself.

Suddenly, Sarah was present and I reached for her reflexively, as one person reaches for another in an emergency. "Where is the calm in this place, Sarah? I don't like it here. Life and death don't coexist here. Sarah, help me!"

"The calm is in you," she replied. "You will find it. Look to yourself. Be real, your honest self."

"Hi Mom!" I said to my mother who was waving at me as I entered the room.

"Hi!" she stammered back, smiling a sincere but oddly sideways crooked smile.

One of my uncles had arrived from across the country and was standing by the bed talking with Jon. Zach was leaning over the bed on the other side, his head on his grandmother's chest. She was stroking his head.

He lifted his head and said, "You look good, Grandmom!" then laid his head back down.

Raising his head once again he said, "Dad sends his love to you, Grandmom."

My mother's eyebrows furrowed; she contorted her face and said in fragmented sentences that she thought his mother was confused and she disapproved of his mother's judgment, meaning your mother should not have divorced your father.

I thought I was going to faint. I held the side of the bed. I wanted to run, or puke, or just disappear. I could not believe that my dying mother, with whom I had enjoyed so many heartfelt, loving, understanding conversations since my divorce, was talking like this to my son. I hoped that Zach did not understand his grandmother. He did not seem to. He simply said, "I love you, Grandmom," and caressed her hand.

Then everyone left. They had been there while I was crying in the bathroom and, for reasons I was not aware of, decided to leave the room. I was left alone with my mother.

I went to her immediately, tears welling in my eyes, and embraced her. Inches from her face I choked out of my constricted throat, "I love you so much, Mom. Thank you for always trying to understand. I know I have made decisions that you don't agree with and that have been confusing to you, but I did what I thought was right, Mom. Thank-you for hanging in there with me."

I was sobbing. My mother was holding me, stroking my head. "Oh honey, oh honey," she said, completely with me in the emotion of the moment but unable to communicate with words.

"We must be honest now, Mom. Now is the time to be honest," I said to her.

"Yes, I want that, we need to be," she replied, slowly articulating the words as if they were connected directly to her soul.

I was aware of our audience of other patients and I was embarrassed, but the need to connect with my mother outweighed the embarrassment. My mother's brother walked in. I looked up at him, my face streaked with tears. "Oh sorry. Just stopped by. I'll come back later," he stammered and then left.

I knew that I was a player in a dramatic scene between a daughter and a dying mother. I was being honest with my mother because we had run out of time. This was not someone else's life I was watching. I could feel the reality of the present as if it was sculpted out of every loving, painful, boring, exciting, angry moment of our relationship. All of those millions of moments existed right then.

"I love you so much, Mom," I said.

She cried.

This was the only time I had ever seen my mother cry. I rarely had told her I loved her. We held each other. Her crying stopped and we continued to embrace.

The others arrived at the door and walked in, unaware of what they were interrupting. Zach went again to his grandmother and hugged her. She cooed her love for him. Corey stood at the side of her bed silently watching. His grandmother looked at him and smiled. He positioned himself in front of me and took a step back. I put my arms around his chest.

Later that afternoon we were informed that the doctor would talk to us in the family gathering room. I told my children what was happening and gave them the option to be there or to watch T.V. elsewhere in the hospital. They both said they wanted to be at the meeting to know what was happening with Grandmom. The doctor arrived and looked at my children.

"I don't think the children should hear this," he said seriously.

I was shocked. I felt like a mother lion confronting a man with a gun in the jungle. "They know she will die soon," I said. "There is nothing they could hear that is worse than they already know."

The doctor looked surprised. I had used the "d" word in front of my children.

"I don't know," he persisted. "What I have to say is not very pleasant."

A surge of anger rose in me. I tried to keep my temper. I turned to my seven year old. "The doctor is going to talk about how Grandmom is very sick and will die soon. You have the choice to stay here and listen or go somewhere else if you don't want to stay."

"I want to stay."

The doctor looked at me furtively. He seemed hesitantly convinced that he would not win this battle and might as well proceed. I put my arms around my sons. Each snuggled into one of my shoulders. They remained quiet and intent throughout the meeting.

The doctor repeated what we already knew. Very large tumor. Both sides of the brain. Surgery not possible. Team will assess possibility of other treatments. Purpose of other treatments is to prolong life awhile.

No cure possible. Length of life hard to know. A year at the outside. I glanced at Mary and then at Peggy who caught my look. There was no possible way Mom would live a year, we both knew that. Tell us the truth. Someone, maybe me, said it seemed more like she had a few weeks or, at the most, a few months. The doctor agreed this was possible.

"Has anyone talked to her about what is happening?" someone asked. The question lit a fire in my head. I burned with the thought that she was dying and no one had told her. Sarah was with me, inside of me, propping me up when I wanted to collapse. Who will tell her and when will she be told? I wanted to know.

Before I asked, the doctor said, "No one has said cancer in her presence." The fire exploded. I screamed internally as loud and deep and long as a victim of violent crime.

"No, she should not know yet," I heard someone say.

"Yes, we agree," someone else said. "No one say cancer around her. Make sure the nurses know."

What is happening? I could barely breathe. She has to know. How will she do all the work of dying if she doesn't know she is dying? Oh, God, this can't be happening.

I finally spoke. "I really think she needs to know. Someone has to tell her. We need to decide who that will be."

No one answered. After a moment the doctor continued as if I hadn't spoken. I felt like I had been injected with a paralyzing agent. Nothing internal or external moved. All I could do was sit with my arms around my children. The first return of motion was internal. "This is wrong," I said over and over silently to myself. Sarah was there holding me.

—23—

Peggy slept in the upstairs bedroom that had been hers growing up. I slept with the boys in the other upstairs bedroom that had been mine. The morning after we arrived, the boys were playing and Peggy and I were sitting on one of the beds talking. The topic was what Mom knew about her illness and who should tell her directly what was happening. We agreed she must know everything.

Jon came upstairs to find us. He wanted to talk too. I told him what we had been talking about. He was defensive, as if we were judging him and Mary for not being more honest with Mom up to this point. I told him this was not about judgment or what should have been done but rather what was important to happen now. Mom needed time to find peace with death.

Jon disagreed. He resented that Peggy and I seemed to be taking over. He had been here all along. He didn't think that Mom wanted to know. Our voices rose in anger.

"I am so sick of not being honest in this family," I screamed. I was shocked that I expressed myself so openly and forcefully. I felt a great swell of love for my mother, like I did when I defended my children. I was not at all sure that I would stand up for myself with such force.

"We *have* to be honest now. She needs to know. She has to know. Telling her is loving her. Not telling is not loving. We have to be loving."

I began to sob. Peggy came over and hugged me. She was crying too. The argument escalated. I said I can't take this and walked out. Peggy left too.

I escaped through the front door without shoes. Anger filled the veins in my head and made them throb. Peggy and I went for a walk around the familiar neighborhood, me doing a barefoot cautious tiptoe dance, Peggy walking slowly with me. As we vented our emotions, we found a calmer perspective. I did not want to go back and face my brother but clearly there was no option.

I walked in the front door. Jon came out of the kitchen and put both of his hands on my shoulders. "I get to talk first," he said. "I just have one thing to say." I wanted to protest.

"You are right. You are absolutely right. She has to know," he said and then walked away.

At that moment I was in my brother's skin, knowing the devastating loss he was experiencing. He could not tolerate telling our mother she was dying because he could not tolerate the thought himself.

My three siblings and I gathered to talk about how to tell our mother about her cancer. All of us could gather around her bed. Her doctor could talk with her. Just one of us could talk. We agreed that if Mom brought it up with any of us, we would be honest. We also agreed to tell the people she was closest to that they should tell her everything she wanted to know. But what if she said she didn't want to know? What if she didn't understand? It wasn't like she had anywhere near her full capacity to comprehend and virtually no ability to communicate. I was furious with this illness that would take her life so quickly and had left her with little mental capacity to deal with it. We decided that when we went to the hospital we would talk with the doctor about how to tell our mother what was happening.

Later that day I was in the hospital room alone with Mom. I had to try to talk with her, gently, softly, cautiously. "Mom, do you know what's going on?"

She looked at me with a serious expression and shook her head, no. She was the frightened little girl and I was the powerful adult.

"You are pretty sick, Mom."

Her eyes got very big. I had never witnessed such surprised terror in another. "I am pretty sick?" she said, not really asking, just repeating, as if she needed to hear the words again.

"Oh God, they are right. She doesn't want to know," I said to myself, shocked at my mother's reaction.

I looked straight in her eyes and she in mine. "Mom you let me know if you want to talk. Now is the time to be honest, okay?"

She nodded and then her expression changed dramatically back to a serene emptiness. It seemed she could not stay with one theme, one strand of thought for very long. I was not at all sure she had retained what we had just said.

I felt foolish and naive. My total conviction that complete honesty was the only avenue was not true. She really did not seem to want to know. I did not know how much was the disease and how much was her personality, but it was clear that blurting out the truth would not be at all what she wanted or needed.

I told Mom I would be back in a minute and left to use the restroom at the end of the hospital corridor. Jon met me half way down the hall.

"It's all set," he said confidently. "I ran into the doctor and I told him we all agreed that someone needs to talk directly with Mom about what is happening. He said he would do it. He's going to talk with Mom later today when he was going to stop by anyway."

Once again I felt like grabbing something for support. I was mildly surprised when I tensed the muscles in my legs and they were strong.

"Jon, I've got to tell you about the conversation I just had with Mom. She doesn't want to know. She's scared and she doesn't want to know. I don't know at all if it is the right thing to tell her everything."

Mary and Peggy walked up and joined us. Part of me felt very foolish. Just yesterday I had been arguing passionately that we needed to tell her the full truth and now I was arguing just the opposite. I was afraid that, because of this dramatic fluctuation, my opinion would be discounted.

I repeated what I had just said to Jon. "I told Mom she was pretty sick and she looked totally surprised and very scared. If she didn't have a brain tumor I would still think she should know, but I don't know what she can comprehend anyway."

We all looked at each other. I felt totally understood and loved. I had no sense of being judged. We were a unified group, struggling with a question we simply could not answer. The answer seemed exceedingly important but we were all caught in the middle of knowing what was right.

"All I can think of to do is keep opening the door and be very sensitive to the cues she gives," I said, breaking the silence.

We agreed to do this. Jon said he would ask the doctor to go very slowly with Mom and tell her only what she seemed to want to know. The next morning another of my mother's brothers arrived. Later in the afternoon Peggy's husband, Brian, and six year old daughter, Katelyn, arrived. Two of Mom's brothers, all four of her children, and all five of her grandchildren had now gathered.

We spent the day taking turns visiting Mom separately and together. We all seemed in tune with one another and with Mom. We told each other our plans for meals and taking care of the children in an easy coordination of efforts all tied to supporting Mom. We agreed that she needed time to rest and time to be alone. The rhythm of meeting her needs just seemed to happen.

In the afternoon I sat outside the hospital room while Mom napped. I poked my head in the door and saw she was awake. She looked at me with an unchanging solemn expression. I was totally taken aback. She had always greeted me and everyone else she loved with jubilance. I walked to her bed and took her hand. She did not return my squeeze.

"You are sad," I said.

She nodded her head slightly.

"You are scared," I continued, meeting her beautiful Scandinavian blue eyes.

"Do you know why we are all here, Mom?"

She continued to stare into my eyes.

"Do you know where you are?" I asked quietly, continuing our eye contact.

"Psychiatric unit," she replied in a sad, anxious tone.

I wanted to cry. I said, "No Mom, this is just a regular hospital. There is something going on with your brain though. You know that, don't you? It must feel very scary. We all love you so much."

I tried desperately to figure out what to tell her. Did she want to know more? Oh God, help me know what to do! I was filled with memory of Sarah. "It will be soon," I heard Sarah say to me. I was holding Sarah, stroking her back.

"Everything is going to be okay," I said softly to my mother. My meaning was that I knew she would be embraced by something good when she died.

"Do you think so?" she replied seriously.

"Oh no!" I thought. "What have I said? Does she think I meant that she will get well?"

We looked deeply into each other's eyes. Mine began to tear. I just nodded.

The next day the doctor told us a group of doctors would decide soon whether any treatment should be given to Mom. We said we thought that had been decided. The doctor said these doctors are the experts and we should wait for their opinion. Chemotherapy or radiation were the options. There was no hope that she would regain cognitive abilities but treatment could slow the progression of the tumor. None of us believed, even for a moment, that we would consider putting Mom through painful treatment for the hope of a slightly longer life. We didn't even have to express it aloud. We all just knew how the others felt. We would wait and hear the opinion of this group of doctors. There was a chance they would tell us something we didn't know.

A nurse told Mary about the palliative care unit in the hospital. Mary walked over and took a look. She came back excited by what she saw.

"There's just a feeling there that is very noticeable. The staff is wonderful. It's very peaceful," she said.

I wondered to myself whether it was like Sarah's floor in the Seattle hospital. "I would like to go see it," I replied.

"Yes, I think we should all go for a visit."

24

Food was a focus of enjoyment for Mom. The cortisone she received to reduce the swelling in her brain increased her appetite. When she ate, nothing else seemed to matter to her. At meal time we gathered around the chair in her room where she sat to eat. Mom's head would stay down looking at her plate as the rest of us talked.

One day her dinner came on a compartmentalized plate. She ate everything down to the smallest scrap in one compartment and then looked up. She looked down at her plate again but did not move her fork towards the rest of the food. Jon leaned over and transferred food from a full compartment into the one she has just emptied. She immediately started eating the transferred food. He looked at me, eyebrows raised. I smiled back my approval of his insight.

One morning when we arrived a nurse told us that in the middle of the night Mom had gotten out of bed and had tried to pull out a patient's I.V. Mary and I exchanged looks of giddy surprise. I giggled stupidly. Our mother did something like that? I was filled with a colliding mix of emotions. Partly I couldn't believe our mother would break a rule. It was like finding out that the teacher's pet cheated on a test. But I was also scared and sad. How much of my real mother was left? How much did she understand what she was doing? She would be horrified to know that she hurt someone. Did she know? Suddenly I was frantic that she not be ashamed of what she had done. I looked to her face and searched for some sign that she was distressed. She was serene and seemed absolutely unaware that anything unusual had happened.

Mary asked the nurse if we could take Mom outside in her wheelchair. The nurse thought that was a wonderful idea. We asked Mom if she would like to go for a walk and she agreed enthusiastically. I was joyful at the idea of taking care of her ourselves, away from the hospital.

Mary, Peggy, and I walked in a clumped procession, Mom in the middle, to the elevator. We took her across the street to a little park. A circular concrete path surrounded its grassy center.

We were delighted to be outside. With children playing in the grass, Mary, Peggy and I pushed Mom in her wheelchair around the path. We stopped at flowering trees and plants and enjoyed each one.

We came to an expanse of bright yellow flowers. Mary tried to remember the name of the flowering plant. "Jeez, I know this one . . ."

"St. John's Wort," Mom stated.

"Whoa Mom!" Peggy exclaimed. "Good one!"

We all congratulated Mom. She seemed pleased and yet surprised at our reaction. She had volunteered at a botanical garden for twenty years, after all.

After circling the park, Peggy, Mary, and I sat on a bench next to Mom and chatted quietly with each other. Mom stared off across the park. Suddenly she tried to stand and get out of her wheelchair.

"Do you want to go for a walk?" Peggy asked, the first person to respond.

"Yes," Mom replied in her slow but clear voice.

Peggy and Mary held Mom under her elbows while I pushed aside the wheelchair footrests. Once free of the wheelchair, she took off at a pace that shocked us. She walked as fast as I would walk if I were in a hurry or exercising. Peggy and Mary still had her elbows. I was trailing with the wheelchair. When we came to narrow parts of the walk, she continued at her fast pace, as her two supports tried to squeeze through. At one point Mary let go, unable to make it through. Peggy and Mom continued.

Peggy teased Mom, "You're like a horse out of the gates, a rabbit out of its tunnel, a fish set free in the ocean!"

Mom laughed but did not slow down.

We made it back to where we started. Mary and I stopped and Peggy tried to slow Mom.

"You want to go again?" Peggy asked, feigning exhaustion. "I can't do it again at that pace, Mom, you youngster!"

Mom laughed and leaned forward, ready to take off again. Mary and Peggy had to go so I said I would stay with Mom and take her around once more.

Something didn't feel right as I walked with my mother around the park. This was not an easy stroll. We were not enjoying each other's company. We were not stopping to take in the beauty of the flowers. She seemed very far away from me. Was she trying to prove something? To me? To herself? She was so determined.

"It's wonderful to be outside, isn't it, Mom?" I said.

"Yes!" she replied, genuinely. For a moment we were connected.

"You have always loved being outdoors," I stated.

For an instant her pace slowed in response and we were connected again.

We arrived back at the wheelchair. "I think it's time to head back, Mom. Let's do this again tomorrow, though. It's so nice to be out here with you."

She drew in a deep breath and exhaled, "Yes!"

"We will come back tomorrow, Mom," I said smiling as I checked the wheelchair brakes, helped her to sit, and adjusted the footrests.

As I pushed my mother to the corner and waited for the light to change I was acutely aware of the passage of time. This beautiful summer day in Vancouver could have been twenty-five years ago. There was nothing about the sky or the breeze or the mountains across the bay that had changed. I could be walking back from the tennis courts with Dad. Mom could be gardening when we arrived home. We could prepare our own lunches and then gather on the back porch to eat. Mom could ask how the tennis went. Dad could tease me about how far I had to go to beat him. I could say I could beat him any time but I don't want to hurt his feelings. He could laugh. Mom could say, "Oh, you two!"

The light changed. It was time to react, to maneuver the wheelchair down the curb and push my dying mother back to the hospital. I was thirty-eight. My oldest child was almost as tall as I was. I never played tennis any more. I watched my kids play sports.

The air felt like silvery mercury as I pushed the wheelchair across the street, parting and rolling back as we advanced, then silently rejoining in our wake. I could not leave so much behind. There was nothing else to do.

25

"We should take Mom to the park tomorrow and have a picnic," Mary suggested when we sat down for dinner.

"That is a great idea!" we said in a chorus of agreement. One by one we announced what we would bring to the picnic.

The next day we wheeled Mom to the end of a picnic table and spread everyone's contributions out on the table. We were an animated group. We all had a sense that this was exactly the type of activity that Mom loved: a family gathering outdoors on a beautiful day. I craved evidence of her enjoyment of our picnic as I looked over at her. She smiled absently, and I forgot for an instant the reality of her large, deadly brain tumor. Then her eyelids lowered, her shoulders slumped, and her hair fell forward into her eyes in a disheveled mess. I could almost hear the "thud" inside as the momentary illusion vanished and I landed fully present in the reality of the moment. I looked around the picnic table and wondered how we would all relate to each other after Mom died.

Bees wanted our food. It was impossible for the children to heed adult advice to ignore the bees. The picnic took on an increasingly agitated air amidst the children's animated cries of excitement and the swinging of young arms as the bees landed on peanut butter sandwiches and soda pop cans.

"Let's get Mom out of here," someone said.

One group, including Mom's two brothers, pushed Mom to a bench at the other end of the park. The kids took off to play baseball in the park's grassy center and the rest of the adults cleaned up. After everything was put away, I agreed to join the baseball game.

During a lull in the game I walked over to Mom. She was beautiful, looking straight ahead, alert and serene. I turned to my twin sister who was holding Mom's hand.

"She's having a great time out here," Peggy beamed. "She loves watching you all play."

"You like it out here don't you, Mom?" my sister asked.

"Yes," our mother replied, drawing out each sound in a slow but clear response. Her eyes twinkled as she smiled.

I squatted beside her and took her other hand. "Those boys are getting better, but I can still beat 'em."

She laughed and tried to say something that came out totally garbled.

"Yeah, yeah, I know. It won't be long 'till they'll be beating me, darn it all."

She laughed again, nodding her head in agreement. We were having a conversation not of words but of meaning known to both of us. She was saying, "You are my tomboy daughter and I like that about you. I was a tomboy too, you know." And I was saying, "My kids love sports just like I did, and I enjoy their sports just like you did when I was a kid."

The children called me back to continue the game.

"Looks like the game's starting again, gotta go!" I said to Mom. She squeezed my hand and I said, "Love you, Mom," as I jogged off.

After a few minutes I noticed that my uncles were hugging everyone and saying goodbye. They had to leave to go back home. One of them walked over to me and hugged me tight. He could barely talk.

"You all are doing a good job," he managed to say through a constricted throat. "I'll be in touch."

I was stunned. I realized that my mother's brothers were saying goodbye to their sister for the last time. I had always known my three uncles as successful professionals, each with a Ph.D., one in Sociology, another in Mathematics, and the third in Chemistry. Now all I could see when I looked at them were family portraits from the childhood they had shared with my mother: the five siblings lined up neatly, oldest to youngest . . . my uncles on their bikes . . . the kids sailing their little boat at the northern Minnesota family lake place . . . my mother swinging upside down on a tree branch . . .

The other brother walked over, wiping his eyes, his face contorted in an effort to control the tears that threatened to take over. He hugged me tight. "Bye," was all he could say. The brothers walked to their car together.

The kids wanted to know why I wouldn't keep playing. I told them I felt too sad to want to play. They accepted this answer without complaint, and I heard the game resuming as I turned and walked back to Mom.

26

The day after the picnic I was the first to arrive at the hospital. The others would come soon. It was another beautiful clear morning and I asked Mom if she would like me to take her to the park. She said, "Yes!" enthusiastically and immediately began to peel the covers off her bed in an effort to get up. I pushed the wheelchair over to her bedside and she got in. On the way out I told the nurse what I was doing and asked her to please tell the others when they arrived.

Mom and I were a happy pair. Mom was alert and calm. I was glad to be alone with her. I pushed her to the elevator, through the front doors of the hospital, across the street to a group of benches in the park and maneuvered the wheelchair so that when I sat we faced each other.

For the first time I felt the stillness I had experienced with Sarah. Mom too seemed totally present in the moment. I had never met my mother on such equal terms. We held hands and looked into each others' eyes.

"Is this a confusing time for you, Mom?" I asked quietly.

She nodded, "Yes."

"Yeah, I bet," I replied.

"Do you know what's going on?" I asked.

"Death," she replied with an expression of deep sadness, her eyes still focused on mine.

I opened wider inside.

"Yes," I said.

We continued to look into each other's eyes. What was real was her loss, her letting go of the life that she had always engaged in so fully. I felt limitless in being with her loss. I was surprised there was room in me; I had felt so completely full with my own loss. I realized that the part of me that was open to her loss was infinitely more expansive than the part that had been absorbed in my own loss.

"Do you want to go home?" I asked, surprising myself with the question.

"Yes," she said sincerely.

I nodded in reply.

We looked at each other in silence.

"How about if I push you around the park?" I asked smiling.

She returned my smile.

Timed by the rhythm of my steps as I strolled around the park, I walked away from the immediacy of the intense emotions I had experienced since her diagnosis. As my entire being suddenly seemed to relax, I understood with great relief that my mother's death had nothing at all to do with my feelings or with my readiness for this loss. My feelings were connected to me; her death was connected to the Whole. I gave my mother's death back to her.

Later that day the team of doctors announced what we already knew: no treatment was possible. I felt like laughing when the doctor, all serious and professional, told us the team's conclusion. We were so much more in tune with our mother than were the doctors. Maybe this was because they hadn't known Mom before her illness so they didn't know what a remarkably intelligent person she had been. Maybe it was their discomfort with a situation they could do nothing about. Their opinions seemed irrelevant to me.

The decision to bring Mom home emerged naturally over the next three days and we began to garner support for taking care of her at home. We could have a caretaker most days, and a nurse would stop by periodically. Pain medication would be prescribed. We could rent a hospital bed, a bedside toilet, and a wheel chair. Supplies such as sheets and pads and adult size diapers could be purchased at a hospital supply store. Mom had to undergo a few more tests before leaving the hospital, which would take a few days. We would need that time to get prepared.

I could not be present for Mom's arrival home but I returned that evening to stories of joy. All who had witnessed her homecoming were filled with pure delight at her reaction to seeing the house, being helped up the stairs, sitting for a meal at her dining room table, and watching Jeopardy, her favorite television show, with the rest of the family. This was right we all agreed; she needed to be home.

27

We sang often to our mother. My brother, with his guitar and beautiful voice, would lead with the rest of us joining in, harmonizing when we could. It became obvious to us very quickly that Mom's long-term memory was much more available to her than her short-term memory. So we chose Christmas carols, nursery rhymes, and hymns. She never seemed to tire of our music. As long as we were singing, we were all connected to each other.

Cards arrived every day. It became a ritual for us to bring them to our mother. We would give her a card still in its envelope. She would take the envelope eagerly, turn it over, and stroke it with a finger. Then one of us would help her open the envelope. She would seem to resent our help slightly until she pulled out the card. As if communicating with a beloved, she would talk emotionally to the card, open it, stare at the words, close it and look at the picture on the front, and then open it again. We learned that she could stay with one card for a very long time, often until she fell asleep, card in hand. It seemed that she knew the cards were sent with love and she embraced each one with uninhibited joy.

One afternoon, a few days after she returned home, I was sitting quietly with Mom as she lay in bed when, in a startled moment, I remembered a brief segment of a conversation from years earlier when Mom had visited my family. As a toddler, my son had loved to sit on the landing halfway up our staircase. He would bring his toys and play, suspended halfway between the upstairs and downstairs floors. Mom had told me that watching Zach play on the staircase reminded her of a favorite A.A. Milne poem. The poem, she had told me, was written for little Christopher Robin to comfort him after his mother died.

"Mom, do you remember telling me a long time ago about an A.A. Milne poem that you really like about a boy sitting halfway up a staircase?" I asked out of the blue. "How about if I try to find it and read it to you. Would you like that?" I asked.

"Ummmm," she replied, as if savoring the thought.

I knew where her collection of A.A. Milne books were on one of her many bookcases and I brought them all into her room. As I thumbed through the books, I read her the familiar lyrical poems that seemed to sing to both of us. Some I read over again as we delighted in the mellifluous sounds.

"Here it is!" I said excitedly when I found the poem I had been looking for. The picture on the opposite page of a sad little boy sitting on a stair in the middle of a staircase was colored pink by a young child's hand.

"It's called 'Halfway Down.'"

Halfway down the stairs
Is a stair
Where I sit.
There isn't any
Other stair
Quite like
It.
I'm not at the bottom
I'm not at the top;
So this is the stair
Where
I always
Stop.
Halfway up the stairs
Isn't up,
And isn't down.
It isn't in the nursery,
It isn't in the town.
And all sorts of funny thoughts
Run round my head;
"It isn't really
Anywhere!
It's somewhere else
Instead!"

"Again?" I asked quietly when I had finished. She barely nodded in response, she was so transfixed by the poem. Somehow these words captured everything. We were all sitting in the middle of a staircase, "not being anywhere but somewhere else instead." Over and over and over I read the poem, Mom staring ahead, completely still. She finally looked over at me and I closed the book.

"I remember when you told me about this poem," I said. "It says a lot, doesn't it?"

She didn't respond.

I will read more later. "Yes," she replied.

In addition to a wonderful caretaker who came over and helped with household chores and meals, a registered nurse stopped by periodically. We learned a lot about taking care of Mom by watching the nurse: how to turn Mom and put pillows under different parts of her body, how to change the bed with Mom in it, how to massage her legs and arms to keep her blood circulating, how to give her a sponge bath.

Despite professional guidance, taking care of Mom's physical needs never became routine and easy for me. I rarely got beyond some level of uneasiness. The rules of privacy changed so drastically. Also, we all struggled at times with feeling confident that we were providing Mom with all the care she needed: Does she need to be moved more frequently? Does she need more liquid? Different food? Is she in pain? How will we know if she is in pain? At times the questions reached crisis points, and we wondered whether we had made the right decision bringing her home. After the crisis passed, however, we would always know that our questions stemmed from our insecurities, and that Mom was where she should be.

My friend Linda, with whom I had shared so much of the experience of Sarah's illness and death, came to Vancouver for a nursing conference at the university after Mom had been home almost a week. I picked Linda up after her first morning of conference sessions and took her to visit Mom.

"Hi Fran!" she said, walking into Mom's room and immediately reaching for Mom's hand with the confident air of a professional caretaker.

Mom smiled, squeezed Linda's hand, and returned the greeting in a garbled but sincere response.

Later that day Linda asked Mom if she would like a really good sponge bath. Mom nodded an eager "yes" in response. Linda went about the task with amazing efficiency and effectiveness, making Mom feel comfortable and at ease.

After the bath was over and Mom was resting in clean clothing, between newly changed sheets, Linda said, "So how was that, Fran?"

Mom's response was to create an "a-okay" circle with her thumb and forefinger which she waved happily at Linda.

The routine for taking Mom to the bathroom was for two people to walk her to the toilet, one supporting each elbow. After she was done, each person would help her stand and walk her back.

One afternoon I volunteered to stay in the house while Mom was sleeping so the others could run errands. Mom woke up needing to go to the bathroom.

"Do you think we can do this by ourselves?" I asked, sincerely worried that it was a lot to handle alone. She chuckled good-naturedly and nodded her head yes.

We made it to the toilet easily. Once she was ready to stand, I supported her elbow but she could not pull herself up. I backed up a few steps to assess the situation and she looked at me and laughed.

"Well, this is a bit of a predicament!" I said chuckling.

"Okay, we can do this," I said as I wrapped my arms all the way around under her arms, my face buried in her neck. For a moment I hesitated as her smell, so close to me, aroused a primal part of the brain that attaches children to mothers and mothers to children. I could feel a deep ache of family, as if the roots of belonging to this group crawled under my fingernails, wove through my joints, between and around tendons, eased through my blood and attached somewhere so core it was nameless. Then I pulled up and she stood, laughing. Once standing, the stench of sour, sick urine and the need to pull the velcro ends of her protective diaper together became all that was real.

"You did great, Mom!" I said, sincerely proud of the effort it took on both our parts to get her from sitting to standing.

She smiled sideways at me, as if she had a secret. Then she turned her shoulders square to the counter and, with a bit of toilet paper she had held on to, began wiping the sink in small, exact circles. Periodically, she would dab the bit of paper up against the faucet end to catch a drop or two of water. Circle, circle, dab, dab. I stood and watched her being totally absorbed in this task and wondered how long she would circle that bit of paper and dab for a faucet drip had I been willing to wait.

By the end of the first week at home, she could no longer walk to the bathroom. We would push her wheelchair to the bathroom entrance and help her walk the few steps to the toilet.

The very last time we took her to the bathroom was an exhausting team effort. She was too disoriented and weak to understand she needed to walk towards the bathroom door to return to her wheelchair. I had resorted to hugging her around her waist, belly-to-belly, and taking tiny steps backwards with my sisters supporting the wheelchair.

"The eyes of Texas are upon you, all the live long day," I had sung softly as we shuffled in our slow procession the few steps back from the toilet. My sisters had joined in and my mother had hummed fragmented notes of this favorite tune.

This is the last time she will use the bathroom. She needs a catheter. Jesus Christ, how can a person use the bathroom for the last time? I thought in-between encouraging exchanges of smiles with my sisters and "The Eyes of Texas." The fact that my mother would die soon seemed much easier to absorb than the fact that she would never again pee in that toilet that had always been there, next to her room.

28

I could not have imagined going to Vancouver without my children. Their grandmother had played a very large part in both their lives and they loved her completely. She was a mainstay in their lives. Every holiday, even Halloween and St. Patrick's Day, was marked by a card from Grandmom. Since we had moved to Eugene, she had taken the train down from Vancouver many times. A visit from Grandmom was an occasion to anticipate eagerly. She was a grandmother who would play board games and cards and would even sit on the floor and build towers from blocks or scoot cars around tracks. From their births, she had been fully engaged in their lives.

During the week after we arrived, when Mom was in the hospital, the children had visited her often. It was obvious how glad she was to see them and how easy their interaction was with her. After we brought Mom home, the children would often sit with their grandmother, holding her hand. They seemed genuinely unconcerned that their grandmother rarely answered their questions in a way that was comprehensible. They simply enjoyed her company and she, very obviously, enjoyed theirs. Because of this mutual enjoyment, I felt certain that I had done the right thing in bringing the children to Vancouver. However, as time passed and the strain on all of us accumulated, my ability to cope with child care was stretched beyond any limit I had ever known.

I watched, as if sitting in the stands, as I lost my ability to parent the way I enjoyed and took pride in. I had read many research articles on the impact of stress on parenting and here I was experiencing it myself. My reserves were empty and the consequence for my children was a mother who uncharacteristically lost her temper over the smallest event. They accepted my apologies and explanations readily but it was obvious to me that I was operating on increasingly unstable parental ground.

"How about if you guys go back and spend a week with your dad?" I asked after Mom had been home for a week. I promise to call often and let you know how things are going. If you want to come back in a week, you can, okay?"

They agreed with a solemn promise from me that they could come back if they wanted to. I drove half way home and met their dad, then turned around, greatly relieved to be able to focus all of my attention on my mother. As it turned out, they would return exactly one week later for their grandmother's funeral.

—29—

Stillness became as much a part of Mom as her breath. It was very noticeable. Everyone felt it in her presence. Her many friends who came by with flower arrangements that filled the house with fragrance, and with food we ate meal after meal, said how lovely and at peace she was. She accepted and returned the love that was expressed openly by everyone as if the flow of love to and from her was wide open without restraint. Words became less and less frequent from Mom, but they seemed irrelevant to the kind of communication that was available to us. We all spent hours sitting with her, holding her hand, feeding her, massaging her arms and legs. We rejoiced in knowing our mother so fully, without the defenses and barriers of most human relationships.

As time passed, the veil between life and death became thinner and thinner. One day I was sitting in Mom's room when she began to have a highly animated conversation with a picture of angels that hung on her wall. The language was incomprehensible but the sense of two-way communication was very strong. After a full few minutes of talk, she suddenly became silent but continued to focus intensely on her invisible partners in conversation. Then, after a few moments, as if it was her turn to speak again, she replied with strong, open emotion, pouring out her heart only to return to the intense silence.

I sat watching, knowing that whatever was happening was between my mother and something that was not available to me. Then she began to get sleepy and quickly fell asleep without reconnecting with me. I left the room and approached my sister Peggy.

"Something kind of weird just happened in Mom's room," I began hesitantly. Then I described what I had just witnessed.

"Oh, you're talking about the angels," my sister said smiling. "It's pretty amazing. Mary's seen this too. We talked about it."

Jon walked up and joined us. "We're talking about the angels in Mom's room," Peggy said to Jon.

"Oh yeah," he replied, "they're in there a lot. Mom talks to them."

"This is too funny," I said smiling. "Here I thought you guys would think I was nuts if I asked about this and instead you're talking like these angels are your pals."

"Well jeez, it's hard to deny something that happens right in front of you," Peggy replied. "I'm really glad they are there with Mom. She seems to need them."

"They are there to help her," Jon added.

"Yeah, they are," I agreed.

After Mom had been home over a week, I decided to go to a Sunday service at the Anglican church Mom had attended regularly. The funeral would be at the church, and I wanted the setting to feel familiar. Sunday morning, on my way to take a shower and get dressed for the service, I stopped by Mom's room. She appeared asleep but her breathing had changed dramatically. She would take in a strained breath, as if sucking air through a long tube. Her breathing would then stop for many seconds. Suddenly she would exhale forcefully. Then the process would repeat. The sound of her breathing was like Sarah's shortly before she died, filled with guttural groans and throaty gasps.

Mary walked into the room. "This is a lot like Sarah breathed before she died," I said softly.

"It is?" she replied, looking surprised and worried.

"I was planning to go to the church service this morning but I don't want to now," I continued.

"When is Aunt Dot getting here?" I asked.

"Tomorrow morning," Mary replied.

"Oh God, I hope it's not too late!"

Peggy came in the room, looked at Mom and then at us.

I motioned to leave the room. "I'm not going to church after all. This is how Sarah's breathing was before she died," I repeated.

"Do you think she's in pain?" Peggy asked, with an expression of great concern.

"The breathing is so hard to listen to because it sounds painful but her expression doesn't show any pain," I replied.

"I'd feel a lot better if we got a nurse or a doctor over just to make sure," Peggy said.

"I agree," Mary said, joining us.

By the time the nurse arrived, Mom's breathing had changed completely back to normal and she was once again conscious and present with us. We described what the breathing had sounded like and the nurse explained that a subtle shift could affect parts of Mom's brain such as her respiration center, then another shift could relieve the pressure on that part of the brain. The nurse reassured us that Mom had no signs of being in pain and that it was very unlikely that she had been in pain earlier either. The tumor had most likely destroyed the pain center in her brain.

I sat with Mom for a long time that afternoon, holding her hand. Once, when her eyes were shut and her breathing was slow and regular, I tried to gently unlock her hand from mine. With her eyes still closed, she tightened her grip. I looked at her face and her eyes opened just a crack. She did not want me to go. I shifted in my chair so that I could rest my head on her bed.

After awhile Mom fell into a deep sleep, and I removed my hand from hers. I continued to sit by her bed, each moment measured by her steady slow breathing. My eyes wandered around her face. She looked different than any memory I had of her: the serenely beautiful face of a porcelain doll, without flaw. I leaned back in my seat and rested, aware only of my mother's rhythmic breathing.

Then, as if injected with a powerful sedative, I began to sink into time. Everything slowed. I became aware of each minute movement involved in emptying and filling my mother's lungs: muscles contracting to pull in air, air being forced down the wind pipe through intricate bronchial branches to lungs, lungs expanding and filling then collapsing as air, undulating with microscopic droplets of moisture, releases.

I sank deeper. Seconds seemed to linger, lazily drifting together. It was during these moments that I experienced a flash of the boundary that separates life and death. In that flash, I saw that the boundary has no substance; it is not real. Something of us is unchanged by life or death.

My response was to stand up mechanically and leave the room. I remember, as I walked down the hall to the kitchen, my sister calling out a question about dinner. I also remember thinking how many times over the last year mere sparks of what is called time had changed my life.

30

Aunt Dot arrived the next morning from Tennessee. One of her brothers had come the day before and volunteered to pick her up from the airport. Her arrival marked a resting point of sorts for me. All of Mom's many friends had visited. Her three brothers had come. Now that her sister had arrived, the goodbyes seemed complete.

"I am so glad I was able to come out and spend time with your mother this spring," my aunt told me once she had settled in. "Your mom and I had such a good time meeting you and the boys in Seattle. And I was so happy to have met Sarah and her family."

"You know, that was just a few months ago. It seems very odd that things could be so different in such a short time," I said, meeting her eyes that looked so like my mother's.

"Did you notice anything during your trip with Mom that could have been an indication of this disease?" I continued. "I keep thinking about the day we all met Sarah and Patton and the girls at the park in Seattle. I remember thinking at the time that Mom wasn't being very communicative that day. I knew she wanted to get to know Sarah because we had talked so much about her but she really didn't interact very much. I thought that maybe her hearing had deteriorated some more."

"You know honey," my aunt replied, "I really didn't notice anything different about your Mom during my trip. We had a wonderful time talking and visiting different people. Let's go see how she's doing."

Patton and I had kept in touch by phone as he and the girls traveled around the country.

"Something's come up," he said during one of our conversations. "There's an interim job for a priest in a small town in Mexico. It would be for about a year and a half. I am strongly considering it because I think it would be a very good place for the girls and me to be as we grieve and recover from our loss. It would be hard for me and the girls to be away from you for that long though."

Tears immediately surfaced as I thought about dealing with yet another loss. "It would be hard for me too, but I do understand your need to be away and to grieve."

"If it's okay, we would like to come see you in Vancouver. It would take two or three days to get there," Patton continued.

Two days later they arrived.

"I know just how you feel!" Hillary exclaimed as she jumped out of the camper van to greet me as soon as Patton had parked.

To my surprise, I found Hillary's unguarded acceptance of the similarities between losing our mothers deeply comforting.

"I know you, of all people, know how I feel, Hillary," I said hugging her tight. "I feel pretty sad. Thanks for understanding."

"Yeah, it hurts very, very much," she said, returning my hug. "I cried *a lot* when my mom died!"

One marker of the progression of the tumor was the amount of time Mom slept. More and more of each day she was not conscious. She also consumed less and less food and liquid. Once the nurse had inserted a catheter, we no longer had the demanding job of taking Mom to the bathroom. Days of constant care taking turned into days of monitoring her wakefulness, waiting for periods we could interact with her and coax her to take a bit of nourishment through a straw.

"We will always remember," I said to her during one of those wakeful periods.

In response, she had become highly alert, nodding her head dramatically, waving her arms.

"We will always, always love you Mom," I continued. "And you know that Zach and Corey know beyond a shadow of a doubt that they have the best grandmom in the whole world!"

She looked at me and with tremendous passion spoke in a garbled language that was not understandable in words. But I knew its meaning: there was nothing more important to her than her family's love.

In between the scattered periods when Mom was awake, we turned our attention to the many details involved in preparing for her death. The funeral. Finances. Her estate. A lifetime of possessions needed to be dealt with.

It was not only Mom's possessions we had to do something with, but also Dad's. Some of his clothes still hung in the den closet. If I buried my face in a shirt and inhaled deeply enough, I could still get a faint hint of his smell. Some of his books and office items were still in the study.

As we dismantled the property that had been my family's since I could remember, the time between my father's death, thirteen years before, and my mother's impending death almost disappeared. I began to grieve not only the loss of my mother but also the loss of the way I had always known my family, its physical objects and place.

At the same time I was grieving loss of family, I began to understand my mother's life differently. In a shoe box buried in a file cabinet we found passionate love letters from my mother to her Yugoslavian fiancee who had been put in a communist camp after WWII. My mother had ached for him. Her love for this person, who was a stranger to me, flowed from her pen as if a swollen river had raged through a dam. In other notes, we found reference to a time during the war when she was working in Washington, D.C. Walking home one evening, she had been attacked, dragged into a bush, and knocked unconscious. A good samaritan had heard her cries and had saved her. We also found a diary that spoke of dreams I knew now would never be fulfilled.

As I had matured into adulthood, I had wanted and tried to know my mother as a full human being. I discovered, however, that it was only when she was nearing the end of her life and I could see her life as a whole, with a unique beginning and end, that I began truly to let go of my narrow perspective of her.

One afternoon, when Mom was asleep, Peggy and I went through the drawers in the dining room hutch. In one of the small drawers, amidst various keys, a deck of cards, and some note pads, I came across an envelope that contained a small round object.

"What's that?" Peggy asked when she saw me trying to decipher Mom's writing on the front of the envelope.

"It says 'ball bearing from orange lazy susan'," I said looking at my sister.

Peggy burst into laughter with me close behind.

"Let me see," Peggy squeaked out, reaching for the envelope.

"Mom! Why did she do that?" Peggy asked, still laughing hysterically.

All I could do in response was raise my shoulders and shake my head.

"I've got to go to the john!" Peggy exclaimed, standing and scurrying out of the room.

I had always known, even as a child, that when my sister and I laughed like this, we were balanced on a ledge. Sitting in my mother's dining room, holding this bizarre envelope, I knew that the edge was a breath away and that my footing was extremely precarious.

There was a part of Mom that I had long struggled with, a part that seemed frustratingly illogical and neurotic. Why go to a doctor you don't believe in? Why save things that have a minuscule chance of ever being used again? Why be so concerned about what other people think? We had found a peaceful truce as I had grown into adulthood. I had simply stopped being concerned about the part of my mother I didn't understand and had focused on the much larger part I greatly appreciated. But here, in this little envelope containing a single ball bearing to an accessory probably in a box on some remote shelf, was evidence of the part of my mother I had struggled with all my life.

And then I fell off the ledge.

I landed in a love so grand and embracing and whole that I knew I had never loved my mother so completely. It was the same love I had glimpsed in the dream with my father and in holding Sarah a few hours before she died; the same love, just a different avenue to it.

I walked upstairs and placed the envelope in the pocket of my suitcase, smiling at the thought of trying to explain to my siblings why I would want this bit of trash: to remember always that it is not the limitations of others that I needed to look beyond in order to love more fully, but rather my own.

31

Patton, all three of my siblings, and I gathered in the living room one afternoon. We conversed while Mom slept in the adjacent room and Hillary and Ivana played in the backyard.

"What time is it, does anybody know?" Peggy asked.

I looked down at my watch. "1:45," I said. As I raised my eyes I saw Peggy's perplexed expression.

"That can't be right, can it?" I replied. "It has to be later than that," my outside self stated while my inside self froze as I realized that, once again, a watch I was wearing had stopped in anticipation of death.

"It's three fifteen," Jon said, looking at his watch.

"My watch must have stopped. That's weird. This watch is almost new," I said, taking it off for a closer look.

I peered up at Patton. "I could try to fix it," he offered.

"I don't think it can be fixed," I replied.

"No, I don't suppose it could," he said as our eyes met in sympathetic understanding.

"My other watch stopped three days before Sarah died, within minutes of the time that she died," I told the group. "Maybe it was exactly when she died, I'm not sure."

We looked at each other in silence.

Jon broke the silence. "It's hard to imagine that life will ever be the same," he said.

No one answered but we all knew that what he said was true.

32

Ten days after we brought Mom home, she stopped eating or drinking. We could swab her mouth, but she could no longer swallow. Her breathing had become increasing erratic. The strain of night care and, more importantly, of worry that Mom would need something we would not be able to provide in the middle of the night, became more than we wanted to take on and we requested a night nurse. Each night we would go to bed comforted in the knowledge that someone was staying up all night with Mom but anxious to know what the next day would bring.

Sunday morning the nurse told us that Mom's breathing had changed frequently during the night. We asked if Mom was close to dying. She replied that it was impossible to know for sure. She could live many days in this state.

But she has consumed very little food or water for almost two days, we said. How much longer could she survive without water? Not many more days the nurse replied.

All day we waited for death, telling our mother how much we loved her. That night we asked the nurse to wake us immediately if there was any sign that Mom was close to dying.

The nurse woke Mary before dawn and told her that Mom's breathing had changed. Mary woke the rest of us.

We gathered around her bed. Over and over Mom would draw in a breath and then stop breathing for what seemed an impossibly long time. Then suddenly she would exhale forcefully and the process would begin again. Each time her breathing stopped, so did ours. Hour after hour.

After lunch I was with Mom alone when her breathing changed again. Her head tilted back, she would draw in a raspy breath, and then, like a machine, release it with a heavy, heaving exhale.

Mary walked in the room. "Get Peggy and Jon," I said to my sister.

We all gathered as Mom's breathing heaved and released. Then her eyes began to tear and she sobbed a few times. On her last breath, a tear rolled down her cheek.

33

A year to the day of Mom's death we gathered at a family plot in a cemetery at the base of Lookout Mountain, Tennessee to bury her ashes. My mother's grandfather had built a large home on the side of Lookout Mountain a hundred years before. Wideview, as the home had been christened, had remained a central family gathering place for generations. At the time of Mom's diagnosis, our extended family had held a reunion to celebrate the one hundred anniversary of Wideview. A year later, when we gathered to bury Mom's ashes, we stayed at Wideview.

"Any chance I could slip away and go for a walk while the kids are playing?" I asked my sister after breakfast in Wideview's basement kitchen. "I could really use some alone time, and I'd like to gather my thoughts for tomorrow," I continued, referring to the fact that I had volunteered to lead the ceremony at the cemetery the following day.

"Sure, go for it," she replied. "Don't hurry back," she called to my already exiting back.

"No problem!" I returned.

"Well, be back for dinner!" she called to me, chuckling.

I saluted quickly as I slipped out the arched screen door to the covered brick porch. It was the first time in days I had been alone, and I savored the thought of a solitary walk.

I made my way along the broad graceful porch to the side of the house and then up the walkway to the narrow road. Across the road, beyond a short brick wall, stood another beautiful home built, like Wideview, within the lifetime of those who remembered the Civil War battles that had been fought on this very ground. As I walked down the road, my hands shoved into the pockets of my shorts, I recalled the Civil War stories I had heard as a child during our summer visits to Wideview. Just as I had done as a child, I wondered which of the trees had been there during the war, which of the rocks had sheltered soldiers, and upon which piece of ground lives had been lost.

I followed the sharp turn in the road towards Craven's House, a famous Civil War landmark. After not more than a quarter mile, I came to the familiar steep staircase up to Craven's House and the surrounding monuments commemorating battles. I climbed the staircase and stopped to read the dedications on some of the monuments. I remembered from a childhood story that the eagle on top of one had been struck by lightening long ago. Shielding my eyes from the sun and peering at the top of the monument I looked, without success, for the missing piece.

We had been allowed to come this far alone as children, but the trails in the surrounding woods had been off limits. I smiled as I approached the carved wooden signs giving directions to the various trails, realizing that I felt a slight hesitation, a remnant of my internalization of the old rules. After pausing at the signs to consider the different trails I could take, I decided to follow the one that ended at the top of the mountain.

The woods were silent in the Tennessee summer heat except for the startling intermittent crescendo of cicadas. I absorbed the silence and was nourished. As I walked deeper into the woods, I could almost tangibly feel the pull of the anniversary, like a gigantic reel pulling me back in time. Soon I was all the way back in Mom's room with my siblings after Mom died. Peggy and I were sobbing into each other's arms, Jon was crying and praying at the foot of the bed, Mary was staring at Mom as if in a trance. Then we were all hugging one another. Peggy, who had been the most resolutely upbeat throughout Mom's illness, couldn't stop crying. I was relieved to see her full grief find expression. Patton entered the room and comforted everyone.

Then I relived the anxiety I had felt when Mom cried as death appeared. I had searched frantically for an explanation. It had seemed that she had seen death and knew what was happening. But why had she cried? The fact that I would never know had felt like a puncture wound between my ribs.

Then I remembered her funeral. Immediate family had sat in the front pew of the packed church. Jon had sung some of Mom's favorite songs, filling the church with the voice Mom had loved to hear. The priest had expressed words of comfort. Mom's friends and siblings had told stories. My favorite of those stories: A year or two earlier, Mom was invited to go out in a ship to view whales. Others decided not to go because the weather was windy, rainy, and cold. Mom went. She returned shivering and soaked. Everyone assumed that she regretted her decision to go. "Was it worth it?" someone asked. "Oh yes," Mom replied beaming, "I got to see a whale."

The friend who told the story had begun in a light-hearted way. Everyone laughed at the loving description of Mom's familiar determination and then at the image of her returning freezing cold and wet. The friend's voice had cracked, though, as she came to the end of the story and there had been a long pause as she gathered herself. "I will miss her," she had whispered before returning to her seat.

Then I found myself back in the present, walking the forest trail.

"What a year it's been since then," I said to myself, as if walking with a friend and clapping her on the back affectionately.

I walked with the memory of the internal commotion I had experienced the past year. Part of the commotion was dealing with what felt like a swirling funnel of loss. One loss was no longer having parents in my life. The main sensation was a blurry kind of disorientation. Like tumbling over and over down a long hill and then standing, it was difficult to find my bearings. Mostly the disorientation was a dull, underlying sense of being somewhere uncomfortable and unfamiliar. Occasionally, though, something would trigger an acute awareness of the absence of parents in my life.

One day I was standing in line at McDonalds when I overheard an older couple ahead of me discussing carefully each item on the menu. When they arrived at the front of the line, they asked the young woman behind the counter detailed questions about the food they were thinking of ordering. All of a sudden, I knew I had to leave quickly. I walked outside, leaving my children to chase after me, as tears streamed down my face. It was my parents' generation in my life that I missed at that moment, someone who treated McDonalds like a real restaurant, who looked at the way things are now and compared them to something different. I missed terribly the steadiness, the wisdom, the groundedness.

The loss of relationship with my mother I experienced separately from the disorientation of no longer having parents in my life. For many months after her death, she was never far from my consciousness. As if waiting in prey for a signal I could not anticipate, acute feelings of loss would occur suddenly, often as a result of events that seemed insignificant: my children's small successes, having pictures developed, wanting to know a detail about my childhood. At these moments, the loss ache would explode and spread in an instant from my heart upward to my throat and face and down to my gut. I would feel stunned when this happened and would function in a kind of numbed trance for hours afterwards.

Sarah's loss I experienced vividly at times through her children and husband and I mourned for them. Other times, I would lose myself in a memory of an image or a discussion with Sarah. I often felt Sarah close by. She would communicate simply that she understood the way things are. Similarly to when we interacted when she was alive, I would feel at peace and present in the moment with her.

The year also held other losses that were like weights tied to my ankles as I tried to extract myself from the suck of the funnel. Patton decided to take the job in Mexico and they left shortly after I returned home. Their absence in my life felt like a wound that would not heal. My mother's house, the place of family gatherings, celebrations, and vacations, sold. I took a trip to Vancouver to bring back the items that were now mine and spent many hours finding places for them in my own home. With this loss, I experienced an odd separation of emotion and intellect. I knew intellectually that the house had sold and another family was now living in it. But my emotional self simply could not absorb this information, and I remained distant from the deep feelings attached to this loss. Then, a few months after the house sold, my beloved fourteen year old dog died. As is often the case with the death of an animal, my grief was open, deep and uncomplicated.

As I tried to explain to myself and others the cause of the tremendous internal explosion I experienced during the year after Sarah's and my mother's deaths, part of the story was very clearly loss and grief. Yet, the core of the explosion was actually something different and much more difficult to explain. Through the experiences of Sarah's and my mother's illnesses and deaths, I had opened to a plane of awareness that was beyond the senses and thought processes that had occupied my life up to this point.

"Stillness" was the word I had found to express to myself the experience of the new plane of awareness. In this awareness, what is real is the vast stillness of the moment. The essence of that stillness is love.

At first, opening to this other awareness felt intensely personal. I knew in some vague sense that what I was experiencing was in the spiritual or religious realm of life but I had no need to define it more precisely. Then one day it occurred to me that the stillness was God. At that moment a giddy giggle rose from my heart to my throat. It was the same feeling I remembered having when I first sat behind the wheel of a car and drove, my father in the passenger seat next to me. "So this is what I have heard about all my life but have never actually experienced!"

Labeling this new awareness "God" seemed very awkward. It didn't fit what I had learned of God as a child. That God was a separate being who watched over me and wanted me to be good. I had thought back then that God must have quite a brain to be so almighty. Even as an adult, most of the portrayals of God I was exposed to were of a separate, judgmental being from whom we arise and to whom we return when we die.

What I found in stillness was not like that God. Most fundamentally, I knew that the stillness was a part of me, and not separate from me at all. Indeed, it had always been a part of me; I had just been asleep to that fact. Unlike the God who hovered somewhere above us all, the stillness I had experienced was here, on earth, everywhere.

I knew this to be true. Being with Sarah and my mother during their illnesses and deaths had been a constant reminder of this truth. It had become as real as anything becomes when you live with it day to day.

And yet, when I returned to normal life after my mother's death, I found myself despairing that what I had known so readily and easily before, I could sometimes not find at all. I became angry at aspects of my life that seemed to block me from this other level of awareness. I didn't want to be in a world so filled with blaming and contempt. I didn't want to deal with my own pettiness. I didn't want to conform to rules that didn't make sense or to achieve in the way that was expected of me. I just wanted to find the stillness and rest in it. And yet I was too engaged in my life to give up the parts that seemed to be in opposition to the way this new part of me wanted to live. And so the different parts struggled and I became increasingly pulled back from the world.

Then, one day, in the midst of despair, I remembered the dream with my father. Suddenly a grin spread across my face and laughter swelled inside of me. It was as if a gust of wind had parted my dark clouds. Like a long-awaited response to a punch line, I suddenly understood why my father had been so amused when he told me that the earth from the heavens mirrors the heavens from the earth, with millions of stars radiating the love that humans experience on earth. The essence of life and death is love. In death, however, unlike in life, there are no self-constructed barriers to love. From his vantage point, it must be pretty funny to witness the degrees to which we humans go to skirt the love we so desire as it sits patiently, always, in our midst.

As I enjoyed this funny image of humanity running around trying to find something that exists under our collective noses, a rush of energy went up my back and I understood that the joke went even deeper: the mirror itself is an illusion. Nothing at all separates anything from this love, not even our own awareness of it.

I had climbed almost to the top of the mountain. A narrow path lured me to a clearing hidden from the main trail. I found a rock formation at the edge of the clearing and settled in to enjoy my private view of the expansive green valley.

Soon my mind wandered to the events of the next day. Friends and family would once again come together in memory of Mom. I thought about the last time we had gathered, at her funeral. I remembered the story Mom's friend had told about the whale. I smiled thinking about how the story captured something I loved about my mother, how she had engaged in life fully and had cared passionately about so many things. Then I saw Mom dying, the tear rolling down her face.

"Why were you crying, Mom?" I asked aloud. The words seemed to carry across the valley.

I closed my eyes and felt the summer heat on my face. My breathing slowed and I sank into the silence. Then, from deep within the stillness inside of me, I heard my mother's voice.

"I cried because I saw the whale. He came to tell me that everything, even death, is about love."